ROUTLEDGE LIBRARY EDITIONS:
POLITICAL THOUGHT AND POLITICAL
PHILOSOPHY

Volume 36

ANARCHY OR HIERARCHY

ANARCHY OR HIERARCHY

S. DE MADARIAGA

LONDON AND NEW YORK

First published in 1937 by George Allen & Unwin Ltd.

This edition first published in 2020
by Routledge
2 Park Square, Milton Park, Abingdon, Oxon OX14 4RN

and by Routledge
52 Vanderbilt Avenue, New York, NY 10017

Routledge is an imprint of the Taylor & Francis Group, an informa business

© 1937 Salvador de Madariaga

All rights reserved. No part of this book may be reprinted or reproduced or utilised in any form or by any electronic, mechanical, or other means, now known or hereafter invented, including photocopying and recording, or in any information storage or retrieval system, without permission in writing from the publishers.

Trademark notice: Product or corporate names may be trademarks or registered trademarks, and are used only for identification and explanation without intent to infringe.

British Library Cataloguing in Publication Data
A catalogue record for this book is available from the British Library

ISBN: 978-0-367-21961-1 (Set)
ISBN: 978-0-429-35434-2 (Set) (ebk)
ISBN: 978-0-367-36956-9 (Volume 36) (hbk)
ISBN: 978-0-367-36963-7 (Volume 36) (pbk)
ISBN: 978-0-429-35207-2 (Volume 36) (ebk)

Publisher's Note
The publisher has gone to great lengths to ensure the quality of this reprint but points out that some imperfections in the original copies may be apparent.

Disclaimer
The publisher has made every effort to trace copyright holders and would welcome correspondence from those they have been unable to trace.

S. de Madariaga

Anarchy or Hierarchy

London
George Allen & Unwin Ltd.
Museum Street

FIRST PUBLISHED IN 1937

All rights reserved

PRINTED IN GREAT BRITAIN BY
UNWIN BROTHERS LTD., WOKING

Foreword

As I write these lines my unfortunate country is rent by a grim civil war. Foreign opinion, seeing in the war but what it carries itself in its own eyes, is split into pro-fascists and pro-communists, so that the conflict in Spain threatens to develop into an international war, and perhaps into an international civil war, since the issue cuts across frontier lines.

The situation has no parallel in modern times. The wars of our days have all been fought by nations against nations. If we are to find a precedent for this dramatic duel between two political conceptions, we have to go back to the wars of the sixteenth century. By a striking caprice of fate the country which, in the sixteenth century, stood as the unconquerable bulwark of orthodoxy against the Reformation, is to-day the first country in the West to know the horrors of the new religious war. Now as then, two incompatible ways of understanding life lead the men of Europe to oppose each other across the Continent, threatening it with destruction.

Nor is this the only feature in the parallel. That nowadays the duel is fought on the economic plane, while, in the days of old, Europe fought against itself on the plane of belief, is but the consequence of an obvious historical evolution which has brought down to earth the centre of our preoccupations, once well set in heaven; yet, though the arguments be all about production, distribution, and consumption instead of about free will, the Holy Trinity, and predestination, the substance of the dispute is just as dogmatic—one might well say just as theological—as in the sixteenth century, and both sides approach it in a kind of "totalitarian" state of mind, more obsessed by principles than attentive to realities.

Finally, just as in the sixteenth century, while one side stands for authority and the other side claims to stand for liberty, the true sense of mental and general liberty is absent from both, so that, now as in the sixteenth century, men of the Erasmian type can but look on and wonder into which of the two abysses their own sweet liberty is to be precipitated.

What does it matter, it might be asked, whether a sprinkling of scholars, thinkers, and scribblers lose their liberty or remain free? The answer is that liberty of thinking in Europe is essential to the future of the world. Two mass movements, as impressive as geological progressions, rise in threatening waves over Europe in utter contempt of any of the real values for which Europe stands in history as a continent apart. Quality, like a graceful ship, carries in its frailty the spirit of Europe. Are we going to let it sink?

The most disquieting feature of the present tempest is the strange attitude of many of the men whose profession and *raison d'être* is that of thinking for the community. Led by a kind of mental inertia to take for granted that all that lies on the left is liberal, many of these men have overlooked the tremendous significance of the abjuration by the masses of that liberalism to which they owe their

Foreword

emancipation. The intellectual sympathizers with communism have not been deterred by the explicit contempt for liberalism in general, and for liberty of thought in particular, which is one of the few features of communism to be found both in its theory and in its practice. They do not seem to be in the least perturbed by the obvious subversion of values implied in the deliberate humiliation of the mental worker considered by communism as the auxiliary of the manual worker; and even now, after so much experience, they go on cheerfully confusing the issue not only between communism and democracy, which is bad enough, but between communism and liberty, which would be comic if it were not tragic.

We are asked to believe that the issue is between fascism and communism, and, in the name of democracy and liberty, we are bidden to espouse the cause of communism. But in these pages we have endeavoured to prove that the issue between fascism and communism is as irrelevant to political sanity as that between Protestants and Catholics is now seen to have been to religious sanity. In the sixteenth century it looked very much as if Europe would have to become either Catholic or Protestant. Yet England, in the end, refused to be locked into this iron dilemma. She struck a line of her own, picked up from both sides all the beliefs and dogmas which she found soluble in her salt-water common sense—and saved the freedom of the world. By showing that the issue was not merely between two forms of religion, that it admitted other solutions,

Anarchy or Hierarchy

that there was no reason why every nation should not adopt her own peculiar way of praying, she made it possible for the two religious parties which threatened to destroy each other and Europe with them to live together, at first in enmity, then in mistrust, later in mutual tolerance; till finally Europe lived down the question altogether, so that the religious differences between Europeans have come to be but one of the elements which add wealth and variety to our mental landscape.

May we now hope to have the same good fortune? Is it possible that the British Commonwealth of Nations, with the United States, the Scandinavian countries, and Holland realize the true import of the issue? While the two huge enemies of liberty—fascism and communism—fight against each other for the right to kill liberty, may not this group of countries remain the bulwark of liberty against either or both of them? This is the only hope of the world. It requires, it is true, that these nations should meet the problems of the day with a daring heart and a creative brain. Just as in the sixteenth century England reformed her Church in a conservative way, so in our own day liberal-democratic countries must reform their public life without sacrificing either liberty or democracy. If they succeed, they will have saved the world from the dismal consequences of fanaticism.

May this book be a not too unworthy offering towards that end.

GENEVA
September 1936

CONTENTS

CHAPTER		PAGE
	Foreword	7
	Introduction	13

Part I
A Criticism of Liberal Democracy

I	Axioms and Postulates of Liberal Democracy	25
II	Ways and Practices of Liberal Democracies	49

Part II
Unanimous Organic Democracy

III	The Principles of Unanimous Organic Democracy	77
IV	The Natural Structure of the Nation	154
V	Methods of the Unanimous Organic Democracy	211
	Index	237

Introduction

BRISTLING with dictatorships, the world is to-day a strange place indeed for those of us who were born and bred under the banners of democracy flapping in the winds of liberty. The citizens of free countries felt then sure to be in the van of evolution, showing the way to those less fortunate men who still lingered under the yoke of Japanese Mikado, Turkish Sultan, Russian Tsar, or even German Emperor or Spanish King. A comparatively slight deviation (by present-day standards) from the canons of justice and respect for the individual struck to the quick the liberal conscience of the whole civilized world. Storms were raised not only by the Russian pogroms but by cases in which the victim was a single individual and the issue, legally at any rate, debatable and complicated, such as the Dreyfus and Ferrer cases, or in recent, incredibly recent, years the Sacco-Vanzetti affair. It was assumed, nay it was known—in fact, nothing else was believed or believable—that the men who lived under standards of liberty below those of France, England, or America suffered from such a privation of one of man's primary necessities, and that a permanent effort was being made by them to secure the full stature of mankind which a free citizenship implies. Of all the anticipations which the men of those days could allow their imagination to make as to the future, the wildest by far never adumbrated that the Russian revolution would lead to a dictatorship as strict as, and more vigorous than, that of Tsardom; that the country of Garibaldi and Benedetto Croce would live gladly and even proudly under the rule of a twentieth-century Caesar, and that the land of Kant and Goethe would vote herself enthusiastically out of democracy within a few years of having voted herself into it.

And yet these things have come, and with an air of leisure and space which suggests that they are not in a hurry to go and that they find themselves at home in the fields of present-day history. Fascist, nazi, or communist movements exist in every nation of the world and find a hearing, a following, cohorts and legions, uniforms, gestures, spirit, and enthusiasm. A fever seizes the world and spots it all over with a rash of coloured shirts. Youth is drawn to these movements by an irresistible appeal which suggests that the spirit of the age smiles complacently on them; and liberty, thus deserted by the grace and force of the young, takes on an old-fashioned air, as if the bright-eyed maiden who but yesterday symbolized her to us had faded into a sallow-faced, toothless grandmother, rather a dear old lady, wandering about, full of strange delusions, in a world which can hardly spare the time to smile at them.

Is this, then, the end of liberty? If so, her reign will have been short indeed. In the ideas of men liberty under the form familiar to us first appears in the writings of a handful of European intellectuals such as Erasmus. In the actions of men liberty's surest steps are the three revolutions—English, American, French. Gradually, through these three

Introduction

conflicts, there emerges a doctrine of the State which is to the old one it displaces as law is to biology. The old State had grown like a plant or an animal. It was organically felt—rather than conceived—by its components. The subjects of the great Western kings—of Spain, of France, of England—did not feel less proud, less manly, for the humility wherewith they kissed the earth trodden by their sovereigns. For them the sovereign was not a mere Oriental despot doing what he pleased—not even when he actually did what he pleased. The sovereign was what the brain is for man, the chief organ of the body politic. No doubt a king could misbehave; the brain can also go wrong. But despotism never was an European doctrine of State, a stable form of government generally acquiesced in. Divine right meant responsibility towards God—the highest and most exacting of responsibilities.

It was in fact the degeneration of absolute monarchy with all that the old regime implied which led to the three revolutions. The divine right of kings, misunderstood by kings unworthy of the crown, led to royal irresponsibility, tyrannous practices, and frivolous governments; the social and economic apparatus became obsolete as the nobility evolved from a class useful for defence to a parasitic class in the State, while the after-effects of the discovery of America and of European penetration in the East dislocated the guild system; so that the old body politic lay in hopeless disintegration when the minds of one of the most intellectual epochs of mankind were drawn by the spirit of the times to dwell on the problem of collective life. It so happened—as happen it would in an intellectual age—that France led the van of political thought and action; and so the biological doctrine of the State was discarded with the dead bodies which it had evolved and, in its stead, a juridical and contractual theory was laid down as the new basis of the State. Men are no longer the limbs of a body politic; they are the subjects of a contract drawn up in order to regulate their political and social relations; and it is this contract which constitutes the State.

The spirit and essence of such a contract is individual liberty. The mind that imagines it—as we might say, that *posits* it—can, indeed must, posit also the moment immediately before the contract is drawn, a moment when man has no obligation and no rights, when he is in fact an absolutely free unit flying unattached in the virginal air of pre-social days. This pinnacle of freedom is man's starting-point in the new doctrine, and from it the individual consents, on his own account, to descend such steps as may be indispensable towards an organization of collective life which may ensure him the safer enjoyment of the liberties left him in exchange for those which he sacrifices. We are no longer in the period when the bolder men wrestled with the monarch for the conquest of this or that liberty; but, on the contrary, in an intellectual stronghold from which we, possessors of our absolute liberty, grant to society such small parcels of it as we think proper. The people, i.e. the sum arithmetic of men, is indeed sovereign.

Introduction

Such is, tacit or expressed, the substratum beneath the liberal-democratic thought which dominates political evolution between the French Revolution and the World War. Wilson fought "to make the world safe for democracy." How strange these words have come to sound twenty years after they were uttered! The war blew like a storm through the nineteenth-century world, and, amid the gigantic havoc left behind, behold the disjointed members of our political constructions. The ways in which the World War sapped and brought down the democratic and liberal ideas of the past century would repay study, for they are many and curious. Perhaps the deepest of them all, that which cut to the quick the roots of the old beliefs, was the searching character of the world experience in itself, the unquenchable thirst for sincerity which it produced in the combatants. War tore away the tinsel and bunting from the garish illusions of men. Nothing so stamps the ex-combatant and singles him out in a group of men as this matter-of-fact attitude towards life in general and political life in particular. Words and ideas are pitilessly stripped of all but the stark reality which they contain. Small wonder that the first words and ideas which had to pass muster before the demobilized soldier should have been those very words and ideas for which he had been told he had fought. Democracy: Liberty: Self-determination.

The statesmen who bear before history the responsibility of the Peace Conference were the solemn harbingers who unwittingly ushered in the new times. They ended the war for liberty filching colonies, the war for self-determination carving about territories on reports from academic commissions, the war for democracy taking decisions on the *fiat* of an autocratic triumvirate. The Peace Conference marks the beginning of the downfall of liberty-democracy, for the three men who thus abandoned the principles on which the war had been fought were three liberal-democratic leaders, and the countries which they represented were the three great liberal democracies of the world. The liberal-democratic faith of the world was first abjured by Wilson, Lloyd George, and Clemenceau.

The eve of the Peace Conference was glorious. Empires fell like packs of cards, and democracies exulted. Great hopes were raised in all hearts, hopes which hailed Wilson with enthusiasm, on his arrival in Europe, as the leader of a new era of liberty. To such hopes the treaty was a tombstone. A great despair passed over the earth, and when its grief died out the world settled down nicely to scepticism, short skirts, jazz, and prosperity.

Meanwhile the war had accustomed Western men to socialism, to authority, and to the supremacy of national over all other interests; three forms of collective life which liberal democracies disliked or, at least, neglected. The sight of bankers raising the price to be paid to them by the State for the money needed to defend their own banks and credit against the ruin of defeat; the sight of armament magnates making huge sums out of the war, of shipowners pocketing fabulous freights for conveying munitions

Introduction

and food, all the unseemly contrasts of "business as usual" with the splendid comradeship of arms made peoples reflect on the opportunities which liberal democracy offers to men of prey; while the extreme complexity of the requirements of the nation in arms taught them a lesson in organic democracy, brought home to them the importance of the expert, the specialist, the leader; thence of order and hierarchy.

And finally the war accelerated the pre-existing tendency towards international organization. A kind of world socialism sprang to life and developed vigorously amongst the allies in such things as coal, iron, corn, and shipping. This organization implied the curtailment of the liberty, till then unlimited, of the business man and his subordination to some national order, itself inserted in the international framework.

These forces, all of them converging against the liberal-democratic system, found a favourable channel which enabled them to make themselves felt. Youth, in particular, was led away from ideas by the lure of sports. A kind of neo-paganism shifted the centre of interest from the mind to the body, from freedom of thought to freedom of ways, from philosophy to motor driving, from silent meditation to the ever-present drone of gramophone and wireless. Thus by the action of apparently external and fortuitous causes the human soul migrated from its inner to its outer zone and evolved a tendency to dwell on the surface. Such an evolution was favourable to the political changes which were in the air, since it sapped the strength of convictions and developed a kind of indifference towards the origins of such new material advantages as the individual happened to come by.

Thus, in Russia, a people which had never known either liberty or democracy paid but little attention to the similarity between the methods of its new masters and those of the old ones, since it hardly knew that other methods existed at all, and the Bolsheviks, at any rate, yielded better results in terms of welfare and education. In Italy the favourable circumstances were, on the one hand, a mass of demobilized men whose absorption back into civil life met with considerable obstacles and, on the other, an exceptionally gifted man; in Germany the change was brought about by the combined effect of a psychology of defeat and an economy of bankruptcy, by debt and unemployment, and by the appearance of a popular prophet and leader.

But neither the drift of post-war tendencies and events nor the helping hand of local circumstances would have sufficed to jeopardize liberal democracy to such an extent if the ideas and systems evolved under their inspiration had been better able to stand the shock. It is significant that the main attacks on the liberal-democratic faith, and the most successful ones, should have come from the left. The herald of the dictatorial era is Lenin, a communist. No one both informed and of good faith can deny that the Bolshevik regime sincerely aims at the good of the people, but the phrase "dictatorship of the proletariat" is a mere quibble. Such a thing is an impossibility, and the Russian dictatorship

Introduction

is of course that of a small party over the nation and of a small group of men over the party. Lenin's imitators hail also from the left. Mussolini, Pilsudski, Hitler began as socialists. Their State sense is closely allied to the communistic sense which underlies all socialism. This fact suggests that, in all these movements, there is a kernel of a similar nature: it may be described as a protest against the weakness of the liberal-democratic State and a vigorous effort at reasserting the rights of the State over those of the individual.

The independent and free opinion which remained in the world could react in three ways: it could yield to the new tendencies, sincerely convinced of their superiority; it could reject them and organize itself for a defensive struggle against them; it could finally study them and, what is more important, study the liberal-democratic system both in its theory and practice in order to ascertain whether it could survive in an unmodified form, or, alternatively, whether it was necessary to revise it in order to give it a new lease of life.

The rhythm of these three reactions, since the days when Lenin opened the era of dictatorships, has been curious to watch. The reaction *against* was strong and general in the first days of the onslaught. Gradually the weaker members of the liberal-democratic forces fell before the charm of dictatorial doctrines: two types of men were particularly caught by the epidemic—the wayward and the hasty-hot. Imaginative and wayward minds, never in any case strongly rooted in any doctrine, crossed the line with a "why not?" and an "after all!" Hasty-hot reformers, too impatient to travel towards the liberal-democratic Arcadia along the leisurely roads of history, took the bold short cut shown them by the energetic sign-posts of the dictators. There remained the bulk of the staunch and loyal. But even on this army the very persistence of the dictatorial systems in several important nations had its wearing effect. To be sure, the devout, the bigots—for there are bigots of liberal democracy—shut themselves the more closely within their faith: yet, in the open-minded, the sight of the rival system flourishing produced a self-critical attitude of the most salutary kind. Too conscious of the reasons on which their political faith stood, too steady to be easily converted, or to be converted at all, to the new faiths, too experienced to be impatient at the slowness of political progress, they were nevertheless too honest to remain obdurate and deaf towards the inner voice which told them that all is not well with the present conception of either democracy or liberty, still less with the practice of them. And thus it is that we find ourselves bound by our intellectual sincerity to examine afresh the axioms and postulates, the ways and methods, of liberal democracy in order to ascertain whether we should not jettison the dead timber which our boat is carrying to save the rest from disaster.

Part I
A Criticism of Liberal Democracy

CHAPTER I

Axioms and Postulates of Liberal Democracy

GENERAL OBSERVATIONS

A DISCUSSION of the axioms and postulates of liberal democracies need not aim at the majesty and elevation of a treatise on the philosophy of government, to be put on the lofty shelves of libraries along with Plato's *Republic* and Montesquieu's *Esprit des Lois*. Nor should it. For its object is not so much to rebuild the foundations of the art of government as to criticize the ideas which circulate in modern democracies and which, in most cases, are to the principles laid down by political philosophers what depreciated paper currency is to gold. Whatever our preferences and opinions as to the way a community *should* live, whatever our political ethics, countries live their own way, i.e. they obey the laws of their own political organisms. The *should-be* in politics is, at best, but one of the factors which go to the shaping of the *is*, or rather, of the *will-be*. Collective life is a natural phenomenon which has its own laws. A scientific study of it could be attempted as a branch of psychology. While other provinces of nature were lost to the scholastics and theoreticians and came under the sway of humbler but more powerful empiricists, collective human life remained, and still is, to a great extent, in undisputed possession of the philosophers, who apply to it their favourite preconceptions. Such preconceptions enter, like everything else, into the general flow of collective life. They are not, therefore, altogether ineffective. They act on some of the human units which go to the making of society, yet they add but little to the knowledge of the facts of that collective life which they aim at regulating. Not till a natural science of collective life has been created, a science more closely connected with psychology and even with physiology than with ethics or law, not till such a science has found its Newton and its Einstein, can we expect to enter into a really human era of history, an era in which collective life evolves—or tries to evolve—according to reason. Till then, collective life will drift along as animal or mineral life, in utter passivity and ignorance of the laws which govern it.

Until that day, still distant, comes, let us at any rate faithfully observe the facts. Let us leave Nature to reveal her laws to us rather than try to dictate our laws to her. And, therefore, let us discuss, not so much the principles of collective life according to this or that author or school of thought, as the axioms and postulates which can be detected beneath the mental and emotional attitudes of the average citizen, journalist, publicist, politician, or statesman. There is a direct connection between the latter and the former, even when the opinions of the general public have evolved in a way which the thinkers who originated them would neither approve nor recognize as their own. But while the principles of the theorist are the source of the mental energy which acts in political life, this energy acts only in the form and in the sense in which it is transmuted and transmitted to the body politic by the protagonists of political life.

This confusion between the theoretical or pure, and the practical or applied, forms of mental energy, is responsible for the intellectual anarchy to which the nineteenth century has led the Western world. The following pages will offer opportunities for illustrating this point with regard to liberty, equality, democracy, capital, labour. In all cases it will be observed that ideas which, in their adequate setting and within certain indispensable definitions, limitations, and reservations, are acceptable to the mind, pass to the arena of public life in a rough-hewn form, stripped of all the qualifications and shades of meaning which had established them as true, in a state which makes them more useful as projectiles for that verbal strife which precedes civil war than as guiding lights to that understanding of collective life which is the only possible basis for peace.

LIBERTY

The case of liberty is particularly illuminating. The intellectual movement which established it firmly in the minds of men was extremely modest in its claims, precisely because the state of things which had provoked it was so backward. Thus Montesquieu: "Political liberty does not consist in doing what one pleases. In a State, i.e. in a society in which there are laws, liberty can only consist in being able to do what one must *will* to do and not being bound to do what one must not will to do. . . . Liberty is the right to do all that the laws allow, and if a citizen were able to do what they forbid, there would be no liberty left, for the others would also have the same power."[1]

As for Rousseau, a convinced democrat, he can hardly be called a liberal. His democratic State is as absolute as the most absolute of kings. This is not yet the moment to discuss Montesquieu's views on liberty, beyond observing that for him it meant the abolition of the arbitrary powers of the despotic Kings of France. Such is the meaning which must be attached to his touchingly modest claim that the citizen must be allowed to do his duty and all that is permitted by law. It is evident that this idea of liberty does not correspond to the subconscious axioms and postulates which underlie the popular conceptions as we find them in our midst. The substratum of the current idea of liberty corresponds rather to an absolute sovereignty of the human being

---

[1] "Il est vrai que dans les démocraties le peuple paroit faire ce qu'il veut: mais la liberté politique ne consiste point à faire ce que l'on veut. Dans un état, c'est-à-dire, dans une société où il y a des loix, la liberté ne peut consister qu'à pouvoir faire ce que l'on doit vouloir, et à n'être point contraint de faire ce que l'on ne doit pas vouloir.

"Il faut se mettre dans l'esprit ce que c'est que l'indépendance et ce que c'est que la liberté. La liberté est le droit de faire tout ce que les loix permettent; et si un citoyen pouvoit faire ce qu'elles défendent, il n'auroit plus de liberté, parceque les autres auroient tout de meme ce pouvoir."—Montesquieu, *De l'Esprit des Lois*, livre xi, ch. iii.

who, from the vantage point of his individuality, contracts away to the State this or that part of his original omnipotence. Whatever the intentions of the political philosophers, the idea of liberty as a mental ferment has given rise to this extreme view, and it is this view, and not the delicately poised opinions of chosen intellectuals, which has shaped political events for over a century. Hence the resentment, the irritation, and at times the revolt, caused by any encroachment of the State—whether justified or not—on the free doings of individuals. This attitude of defiance, which takes for granted that the individual has a natural right to an all-round freedom, is identical in all classes of society. It will be found in the aristocrat, the landowner, the capitalist, the town worker, the peasant. It is a feature inherent in contemporary Western men of all stations of life. Since it is due to an overdevelopment of individualism, i.e. of the centrifugal force of society, it is one of the most disruptive factors in contemporary life, and at bottom one of the most inimical to true liberty; for not only does it call forth, as a reaction, an over-development of authority, leading to tyranny, but, in practice, it always takes the form of an attack of one set or class of citizens against the liberty of another set or class.

There is another current error in connection with liberty which is also responsible for not a few mistakes of liberal democracies; it is generally assumed that liberty is a primary necessity of all human beings. Now this assumption is belied by the facts. Few are the pages in world literature which can be compared with that immortal passage in *The Brothers Karamazoff* when Ivan tells Aliosha his story of the return of Jesus to earth. We are in the sixteenth century, in Seville. Jesus appears, and all follow Him, for all recognize Him at once. But the Grand Inquisitor, an old man of ninety, pale and austere, orders Him to be taken to prison, and comes to see Him in his cell at midnight. There is no dialogue, for Jesus says nothing. But the Grand Inquisitor reproaches Him at length for having returned to the world again after having done so much harm already in his first incarnation. Men are not able to be free. Liberty weighs too heavily on their poor shoulders, and the Catholic Church, more kind and loving than Jesus, draws to itself all the pain and responsibility of freedom and of the knowledge of things and lets men live, and even sin, provided only they accept its authority. This moving and profound presentation of an eternal theme deserves to be meditated on by all men who, by thought or by action, influence public life; for it goes further and deeper than mere politics. It penetrates to the innermost of the human spirit and uncovers eternal truths, illuminated by that passionate love of the human being and that inexorable insight into the deepest miseries of man that make Dostoievsky so poignant. At this depth the problem of liberty becomes universal and frees itself from the shackles of time and space, allowing Dostoievsky to go on to prophesy in the simplest way, and yet with admirable power and vision.

"Oh, ages are yet to come of the confusion of

free thought, of their science and cannibalism. For having begun to build their tower of Babel without us, they will end, of course, with cannibalism. But then the beast will crawl to us and lick our feet and spatter them with tears of blood. And we shall sit upon the beast and raise the cup, and on it will be written, 'Mystery.' But then, and only then, the reign of peace and happiness will come for men. Thou art proud of Thine elect, but Thou hast only the elect, while we give rest to all. And besides, how many of those elect, those mighty ones who could become elect, have grown weary waiting for Thee, and have transferred and will transfer the powers of their spirit and the warmth of their heart to the other camp, and end by raising their *free* banner against Thee? Thou didst Thyself lift up that banner. But with us all will be happy and will no more rebel nor destroy one another as under Thy freedom. Oh, we shall persuade them that they will only become free when they renounce their freedom to us and submit to us. And shall we be right or shall we be lying? They will be convinced that we are right, for they will remember the horrors of slavery and confusion to which Thy freedom brought them. Freedom, free thought, and science will lead them into such straits and will bring them face to face with such marvels and insoluble mysteries, that some of them, the fierce and rebellious, will destroy themselves, others, rebellious but weak, will destroy one another, while the rest, weak and unhappy, will crawl fawning to our feet and whine to us: 'Yes, you were right, you alone possess His mystery, and we come back to you, save us from ourselves!'

"Receiving bread from us, they will see clearly that we take the bread made by their hands from them, to give it to them, without any miracle. They will see that we do not change the stones to bread, but in truth they will be more thankful for taking it from our hands than for the bread itself! For they will remember only too well that in old days, without our help, even the bread they made turned to stones in their hands, while since they have come back to us the very stones have turned to bread in their hands. Too, too well will they know the value of complete submission! And until men know that they will be unhappy. Who is most to blame for their not knowing it, speak? Who scattered the flock and sent it astray on unknown paths? But the flock will come together again and will submit once more, and then it will be once for all. Then we shall give them the quiet humble happiness of weak creatures such as they are by nature. Oh, we shall persuade them at last not to be proud, for Thou didst lift them up and thereby taught them to be proud."[1]

The disregard of this profound truth which the genius of Dostoievsky so admirably brought out has been of frequent recurrence in politics. It has contributed to yet another confusion, that between democracy and mass government, by a failure to discriminate between *inhabitant* and *citizen*, the first a mere unit of population, the second an active participant in public life. Liberty is not a latitude

[1] Mrs. Garnett's translation (Heinemann).

which all men want or require. Political liberty still less so. By granting political liberty to all, to the active as well as to the passive members of the community, democracies have allowed the growth of organizations within which active-minded individuals can wield the accumulated political power of masses of passive inhabitants. Hence the transformation of extra-political gatherings, such as trade unions, associations of ex-combatants, the churches, etc., into direct political forces with detrimental effects on public life.

It is evident, therefore, that liberal democracies have suffered in their evolution from a popular conception of liberty which is both too absolute and too general. Any revision of the liberal-democratic system must begin with a revaluation of liberty which will define and condition it more strictly and will recognize that, far from its being a boon to all men, it is a burden to many.

EQUALITY

When we approach the idea of equality, and compare the way in which it was conceived by the theoretical founders of liberal democracies with the way in which it is understood by the average liberal democrat of our day, the contrast is even more impressive than in the case of liberty. As with liberty, equality was conceived by the political philosophers of the eighteenth century in a reaction against the prevailing state of things, overburdened with obsolete and unjustifiable privileges. For them, equality ultimately meant absence of privilege not justified by some reason which all citizens can approve and understand. But such a balanced and complicated idea, as it fell on the mass, fermented it in unexpected ways and led to a simplified and extreme view of equality, the after-effects of which in liberal-democratic societies have been disastrous.

For it is only natural that the claim of equality, once awakened in the mass, should have developed from an opposition against unjustified social privilege to opposition against justified social privilege, and from this to opposition against all privileges whatsoever—even natural ones. This last stage is of course absurd, since inequalities in talent, virtue, beauty, force, health, or creative power cannot be corrected by man. But the opposition against the natural privilege of those so favoured by fortune is, nevertheless, an important element in the conception-emotion of equality underlying liberal democracies. It is, no doubt, a psychological error, for few facts of experience are better established than the law of compensation which makes human beings pay for their natural assets with some natural liability. Yet the fact remains, and no analysis of liberal democracy can afford to neglect it.

The levelling attitude which it creates accounts for one of the most fallacious aspects of the current conception of equality—that which takes for granted that men are interchangeable, at any rate in public life. Turn to Plato; see the care wherewith he analyses the qualifications which the several functionaries of the State must possess; see with what exquisite attention Huarte defines the moral, and even the physical, conditions for the profession of kingship. In our liberal democracies every Tom, Dick, or Harry is assumed to be apt to perform any public function which may be in the giving of his party, and we take pride in the open-mindedness wherewith we admit to the most delicate functions of government the roughest diamonds—or pebbles— which universal suffrage may throw up.

It follows that, in actual fact, and whatever the theory of equality may have to say, the working of the idea of equality in our liberal democracies has led to the complete disregard of hierarchy, of specialization, and even of natural conditions. Hierarchy is the necessary result of organic specialization. A subconscious opposition to natural capacity, added to a conscious opposition to acquired or technical capacity, has led to an equalitarian levelling down of the ranks within institutions. This is bad enough; but the excesses of equalitarianism have gone further: they have led to the disregard of the most obvious differences between human beings, even those which Nature has rooted in the deepest recesses of life that, for instance, between man and woman, a natural distinction which, with the most persevering foolishness, the nineteenth and twentieth centuries have sought to obliterate with an equalitarian prejudice which has deprived the feminist movement of much of its beneficent effect on the legal and social emancipation of woman. In recent years the excesses of equalitarianism have led to a similar disregard for the natural inferiority of inexperienced youth. The student has suddenly become an important political personage; his opinions have come to be heard, his associations consulted, his decisions feared, as if the student could be considered a full and autonomous unit of civil life.

A worse, perhaps, and a subtler form of equalitarianism afflicts society. It consists in denying, or ignoring, the irrational elements in collective life, all the imponderabilia, the delicate shades of character, the differences which constitute the salt of society. The graces, the arts, the value of fruitful leisure, the creative power of the unexpected, the virtues of luck —all that which cannot be reduced to figures, to rules, or to general laws—is neglected or forgotten by the politically minded liberal-democratic masses. Yet these elements of inequality remain in collective life as strong as ever, and the average human being, unspoilt by politics, holds to them instinctively, even at times against the grain of his conscious opinions, because they belong to deeper levels of life than the merely political.

DEMOCRACY

Nowhere perhaps is the contrast between principles and assumptions more striking than in what concerns democracy. The principle of democracy rests on the vision of a society of enlightened citizens who postpone their lower and more immediate interests to their higher interests, identical with those of the community. Democracy presupposes, therefore, a

Axioms and Postulates

well-educated mass of citizens, well-educated morally and politically even more so than in other ways. And once the existence of such a mass of citizens is granted, the case for democracy is unanswerable. A truly noble sight. Here is a nation in which every man and woman, whether city merchant, shopkeeper, civil servant, domestic servant, field labourer, landowner, member of the liberal professions, or financier, is fully aware of his duties to the State; adequate agencies of information convey to every individual the objective facts which he must know about the coming budget, current legislation, trade relations, the cost of living, the proposed treaty with a powerful nation; the citizens, high or low, study the facts carefully in order to form an opinion on them, and thus be able to judge of the services to the nation of the particular representative they have helped to choose; when their taxes are asked of them, they scrupulously fill up their schedules and punctually pay the sums claimed on their own showing; while, by frequent gatherings with their co-citizens, they keep alive a constant discussion of the affairs of the State. In such a happy democracy the problems of public life are always solved in peace and according to reason, for public opinion is well-meaning and well-informed, while parliament and government are well chosen and well watched over. Every citizen performs his duties to the full and claims no more than his strict rights. Education prepares the co-operation of the coming citizens under the best auspices. Defence is adequate, and never seeks either foreign aggression or internal tyranny. Foreign affairs are conducted with cordial dignity. All is well in the best of worlds.

But what has that to do with democracy "as she is lived"? That such an Arcadia may be in front of us, that we aim at it, is that a reason for assuming that the methods of government which would be possible under it can be applied in our day? The confusion between democracy as a goal and democracy as a method is one of the most tragic mistakes of our times. It is, of course, but natural that government *by* the people should have been fought for and obtained as the only guarantee of government *for* the people. But if and when experience has shown that government *by* the people means not only a bad government and a bad guarantee of government *for* the people, but also a road leading astray from the true way towards government *by* the people, what is there left to say for it? The fact is that not one of the assumptions of the democratic principle resists the wear and tear of daily political life; that the average inhabitant is a bad citizen, unable to see in the collective interest his own higher interest, ill-informed, caught in a mesh of prejudices of class or of religious or political creed, selfish, though at times capable of sacrifice, sluggish, though at times capable of sudden flares of political enthusiasm, usually due to partisanship, hardly ever to citizenship. In these conditions the principle of democracy applied in all its implications leads to the very negation of what it seeks to attain. The interests of the community are lost in the dust of personal and party strife, and would-be democracy remains for ever in sight of the promised land, for ever unable to attain it precisely because, in its impatience, it has mistaken the road for the end of the journey.

Behind this misconception there lurks a deeper one. Democracy rests on the idea of the sovereignty of the people. But what is the people? In the eyes of the theorists, who have reflected upon it, it is the nation organized for collective life, with an adequate distribution of labour and responsibility amongst its several institutions. In the eyes of the average man "the people," in the phrase "the sovereignty of the people," means 15 million votes against 14 million. The difference is bound to appeal to the thoughtful as a political problem of the utmost gravity.

CAPITALISM

The theoretical principles on which capitalism rests, evolved along with the development of modern political economy from the physiocrats to Adam Smith, Ricardo, and Bastiat, may be summed up in two relatively simple ideas: the value of private initiative and a belief in the harmonious adjustment of natural laws which leads to the claim that the State must not meddle in economic affairs. These two ideas were potent sources of social energy during the heroic age of capitalism, and though too close an inspection of the achievements of unfettered capitalism would probably be deprecated by its most enthusiastic adherents, capitalism has on the whole a good ground for pride and satisfaction in that, historically, it did what no other human agency was ready to do at the time for lack of men, spirit, and imagination.

These two principles assumed, moreover, that private initiative was to remain within the limits of private ethics, and that the economic activity which claimed that the State should abstain from any interference was not merely to remain within the limits of common law, but was also itself to abstain from interference in political affairs, and therefore to respect the sovereignty of the State, the sound working of democratic institutions, and the liberty of ordinary citizens.

Are these the assumptions of the ordinary business man? We know that the beautiful harmonics of classical economists have degenerated into a wild business warfare in which the imperative of private interests has displaced all other considerations; that, while the business man resents the interference of the State, he is careful to interfere in political affairs, to influence political institutions, and even unduly to complicate the motives and arguments on which politicians and high officials take their decisions. We know that when business is not doing well the State is expected to intervene in order to save it from disaster, and that, faithful to his subconscious criterium of private interest above all, the business man is to be left alone in prosperity when partnership means dividends, but is free to seek the co-operation of the State in the lean years, when partnership means distribution of losses.

The assumption has thus shifted from the classical

Axioms and Postulates

"Let do, for private interest will in the end mean general interest" to a dry and unrestricted "Private interest first, last, and all the time."

This is one of the causes of the downfall—in many ways to be deplored—of capitalism. That masses of people should give their work for private interest was only conceivable if and when experience showed that private interest was instrumental in developing general interest, that is to say, as an organic force ensuring the automatic and healthy distribution of wealth. But when private interest revealed itself as a disease, over-developing the wealth of some citizens at the expense of that of others, it was obvious that, sooner or later, it was bound to meet with a natural reaction whereby the body politic would endeavour to cure its diseases by destroying the parasite.

This reaction has been invigorated under the influence of another distortion, which ideas on capitalism are apt to undergo. The prestige of capitalism rests on the utility of capital and of the creative power, talent, resourcefulness, and energy of the promoter. No organization of society can do without these two primary elements in the creation of wealth: *capital* and the *capitalist*. They may come to be transformed; they cannot be annihilated. Now both have been twisted round from their original meaning as it is to be found in the classical books into unrecognizable and parasitical notions, which are those that actually circulate and constitute current capitalism; *capital*, which is instrumental wealth, composed of tangible things, animate or

41

inanimate, has been twisted into meaning *money*, which at best is coin and at worst scrips of paper, and in both cases tokens of debt; while the *capitalist*, who, when discussed theoretically in books, is paraded as the energetic, intelligent, and resourceful promoter, becomes in fact the sleeping partner holding capital, i.e. a passive parasite holding scrips of debt. We are not advocating confiscatory measures, nor do we forget the social value of savings and the need of an adequate reward to stimulate them. The time will come to discuss and adjust these matters. We are merely dealing with axioms and postulates, subconscious attitudes and quiet assumptions. And we observe that, while in theoretical principles and books, *capital* means a positive accumulation of wealth and *capitalist* an active creator of wealth, in current and practical fact *capital* means a negative accumulation of debt and *capitalist* a passive holder of debt.

This transformation of the two fundamental notions of capitalism is undoubtedly one of the most important factors in the evolution of ideas away from capitalism. Here is the worker handling the machine, "his" machine, as everybody, even his jobmaster, will say for short. He tends it, knows it, it is his daily companion; he is familiar with its qualities and defects. But it does not belong to him. If at least it belonged to the boss, the man who can be seen working hard in his office, longer hours than any of his men, who is capable of handling the whole works and of seeing the whole business through—but no. When there is something wrong

Axioms and Postulates

about salaries, strikes, and so forth the boss will say to his men, "I must consult the owners. I am not my own master." And even the "owners," who have never seen the machines and hardly know what they are for, at least they know where the works are located. But even they are only the owners up to a point. Most of the money comes from a bank somewhere. That is, the works, the men, the boss, and even the owners are owned by some unknown people. They have a case also, of course, these unknown people. They represent a socially useful element, or at any rate they may do so. But we are not judging, we are describing. The psychological situation created by this contrast between the positive and theoretical, and the negative and practical, conception of capitalism is bound to disintegrate it and to accelerate its downfall.

LABOUR

The labour movement rests on a divorce equally striking between its theoretical principles and the assumptions which are postulated by its adherents. That all wealth comes from labour is a principle which can be accepted when it is duly interpreted, and it generally is, by its theoretical exponents. In its crude form it is not a principle of Marx, who was a good economist, if such a thing exists at all. In the "labour" which produces all wealth several kinds of labour may be discriminated; there is the immediate manual labour of the operative (never, by the way, purely manual); thus, for instance, the physical effort and mental attention of the engine-driver in charge of a train; there is the manual labour accumulated in the machinery, in this case the locomotive, the permanent way, the signals, the stations, etc.; there is the intellectual labour of the experts who calculated and planned all this machinery; there is the mental labour of the accountants, managers, and administrators who apportion the cost between the several economic factors which keep the railway going; there is even the State, its political and general work for peace and civilization which make it possible for the railway to be run; and, finally, there is the tradition of civilized life without which the railway would not exist at all. These elements go to the making of wealth. All count, directly or indirectly, as labour, and when this word has been so expanded as to contain, along with the efforts of the worker, talent, science, capital, civilization and the whole State, we all accept the statement that labour is the cause of wealth.

Such is the reasonable view—and the generally accepted view—as to the relationship between labour and wealth. It is no discovery. It is rather in the nature of a truism. But though no one in the course of a conscious discussion would deny it, or even throw any doubt over it, the fact is that, in the current assumptions of the labour movement, in the subconscious attitude of the adherents to the movement, the "labour" which creates all wealth is the labour of the working man. This is the fact. A process of simplification similar to that which has given rise to grossly inadequate ideas on liberty, equality, democracy, and capitalism has deformed political economy to such an extent that, in the minds of the mass of the workers leavened by socialism, all production flows from the workers' hands, and all its fruits are due to them; therefore all that is not theirs is ill-begotten wealth, the booty of bourgeois robbery. It is evident that such an attitude on the part of workers—a growing mass of citizens—can hardly be said to constitute a sound basis for a State.

This misconception, more or less related to Marx's theory of surplus value, gives birth to a bitter feeling of class because the worker believes himself to be despoiled by the capitalist. Here is one of the most beautiful paradoxes of history: socialism is born and bred from a feeling of ownership. Far from meaning the negation of all property, it means the affirmation of it. The worker is not class conscious because he aims at an idealistic abolition of private property, but because he believes that his private property has been filched from him by the capitalist. Were it not for this paradox, the success of socialism would not have been as rapid as it has been amongst the masses; for human beings are what they are, and few amongst them are those who do not experience the appetite to own things. This, the first and one of the subtlest of the misconceptions which underlie class struggle, explains much of the bitterness of it, inasmuch as this misconception brings into the struggle an element of envy; for the worker who feels inimical to the bourgeois feels so not because he sees in him the representative of a mode of living of which he disapproves, as a Roman might feel against a Carthaginian, but because the bourgeois has got where he, the worker, would like to be. Let us say, again, we are not discussing principles but facts, psychological facts. That is why, paradoxical as it may seem, the bitterness of class struggle does not arise in workers who, being original human beings, having salt of their own, are seldom afflicted by a desire to change class, are good mixers, and feel perfectly happy where they are; but, on the contrary, in workers who hate the bourgeois because they admire him and would like to be one like him.

This explains how class struggle has been foolishly extended to include amongst the classes antagonistic to the workers numbers of people who have nothing whatever to do with capitalism, merely because they live in surroundings and in ways which are not proletarian. Though such a mode of living nowadays includes many members of the working classes, though many working-class people are well off to the point of being in actual fact small capitalists, either as owner-workers or what, from the socialistic point of view, is worse, as owners of shares and bonds, class struggle is still preached and contributes, as few things do, to disintegrate democracies. It is directed against the whole middle class, though the evils of capitalism afflict the middle class as much as, and in certain ways perhaps more than, they afflict labour. It tends to thrust the middle class into solidarity with the capitalist, though by natural affinity their solidarity should induce them to lean towards labour. From any angle from which it may be considered, theoretical, tactical, emotional, or from the point of view of justice, the class struggle is a senseless cry, even when it is not uttered by wealthy socialists. But though senseless, or perhaps because it is senseless, it provides the vital element, the passion of the heart, which is so strong a driving force in labour movements.

CONCLUSION

This brief analysis of the mental attitudes, which, irrespective of the doctrines whence they come, are actually to be found in liberal democracies, shows as a feature common to them all that they tend to disintegrate and disorganize society. Liberty understood as an absolutely individualistic right and extended to many individuals incapable of administering it, or indifferent to the duties which it implies; equality, felt as a levelling agent, inimical by instinct to all hierarchy, to all specialization, to all competence, and even to all natural difference; democracy, transformed from the ideal and normative plane of aims to the immediate and empirical plane of methods; capitalism, left free to roam in search of its prey and allowed to fall back on the State for help when its chase has proved too dangerous; labour, convinced that in it resides the productive power of the nation and resentful of the other classes as despoilers of its own property—all these forces are disruptive, divergent, all work within the State as grave diseases within the body, for all are directed to fostering the interests of individuals or of classes,

Liberal Democracy

but not that of the State conceived as an organic whole. Now the mental attitudes of the several classes of society are the soil in which predispositions germinate, and predispositions are the inner conditions which predetermine the actions of men. It is evident, therefore, that liberal democracies evolve in our day under a strong predisposition towards anarchy.

CHAPTER II

Ways and Practices of Liberal Democracies

FAILURE OF LEADERS

OF all the ways and practices of liberal democracies, that which has been the most effective in bringing them to their present position of discredit is the failure of leaders actually to lead. Despite appearances, liberal democracies are dependent on leadership even more so perhaps than other more authoritarian forms of government; for, in authoritarian systems, the springs of authority are more firmly established at all the levels of the political organization, while, in liberal democracies, their natural tendency to weaken the springs of political authority must be counterbalanced by a higher level of personal and moral authority on the part of their leaders. Now, liberal-democratic leaders can hardly be said to have shown the courage and self-control which are necessary for the acquisition of moral authority.

At the outset it may be said that, through the operation of the set of the current axioms and postulates on liberty, equality, democracy, capitalism, and labour which we have endeavoured to analyse above, liberal-democratic leaders have seldom had a sufficiently clear perception of the organic nature of the State and, even when they have had it, they have often lacked the courage to say so and to act accordingly. Steeped in the prejudices of the day, they have accepted in all its disastrous implications the statistical conception of democracy, i.e. the view that numbers of votes, no matter by whom, how, or on what occasion given, decide the issues before the community.

This numerical or *statistical* conception of the State has had for its initial effect a total reversal of the current of power, through a literal interpretation of the doctrine of the sovereignty of the people. Leaving comfortably asleep on their library shelves all that the best authors have to say on this subject, all their nicely balanced *buts* and *notwithstandings*, politicians go before their electorates and loudly proclaim them sovereign. To them they submit the most abstruse problems of finance, the most delicate questions of foreign policy or of national defence; or else, keeping a discreet silence on these, the real issues, they catch their vote and the delegation of sovereignty which it implies by appealing to their passions, their petty interests, or their taste for drink. Thus a competition downwards becomes the law of political life, and thoughts on government have to be gauged to the minimum intellectual size of the electorate.

This observation holds equally good when from the sphere of political action we pass to that of political thought. Nothing is more striking than the gravitation of intellectuals towards one or other of the two poles of attraction which, between them, dominate the century—either they become servants of capitalism or servants of labour. The phenomenon is more striking with the intellectual servants of labour. Capitalism, after all, in so far as it claims free individual initiative, would seem to be more akin to the individualistic character of the intellectual; there is a *prima facie* similarity of tendency between capitalism and intellectualism. Capitalistic enterprise is not unlike intellectual creation, and it may be that they are but different forms of the same energy. At any rate, many are the capitalists in whom the urge forward is due, not to any material ambition, but to a creative impulse. Nevertheless, the obvious evils of unfettered capitalism in the nineteenth, and perhaps even more so in the twentieth, century, should have led intellectual leaders to a more cautious and critical attitude with regard to capitalism. As for socialistic-minded intellectuals, if their initial impulse may be explained as a generous and human protest against the thraldom to which capitalism had reduced the working classes, it is hardly possible to approve whole-heartedly their surrender of all the duties and dignity of mental leadership, their acceptance of the utterly inadequate doctrine of class struggle, their demagogic flattery of the power, importance and virtues of the working classes, and their passive acquiescence, and even active collaboration, in the contempt for intellectual work which is a subconscious but only too real and active a feeling among the masses.

Few are those among intellectuals who have known

how to remain free critics of both socialism and capitalism; who, convinced that classical capitalism has had its historical day and must give place to other forms of social and industrial life, are nevertheless aware of the incapacity of the working classes to provide the adequate solution for this delicate problem, not merely because they are not competent enough, but because they are not objective enough, not sufficiently able to disentangle the interest of the nation from their own class interest.

The failure of intellectual and political leaders has been, in part, the inevitable result of the liberal-democratic ferments and misconceptions which typify collective life in the nineteenth and twentieth centuries; but it can also be traced to the corrupting effect of power in an epoch of wealth and prosperity during which, moreover, the traditional springs of ethics had given way while new ones had not, have not yet, been evolved. The inherent immorality of our age need not be considered as particularly worse than that of other periods of history; but the enormous expansion of wealth, which is a specific feature of the industrial era, no doubt developed the appetite and capacity for enjoyment in all classes, particularly in the leading ones, with the obvious result that leaders lost much of their moral authority by becoming the prey of power-lust, for the sake of the other pleasures which go with power.

The collapse of democratic institutions which threatens the world will, to a great extent, be due to the cowardliness of leaders, in itself a consequence of their feeling of their own failure as leaders. A leader, conscious of his own value from the point of view both of ethics and of competence, dares lead, he dares precede and form public opinion. But our democratic leaders have gloried in the idea that they have the ear on the ground. Mr. Coolidge went so far as to assert with the blunt frankness which characterized him, that a President who would imagine that he had the right to precede and lead, instead of following, public opinion would be a traitor to American institutions. Far from me to suggest that the upright and taciturn New Englander was corrupt; but when Calvin Coolidge uttered that thought he was, as he so often was, the passive mouthpiece of a state of opinion current in the leading classes, and that state of opinion came to be formed in them by the general conviction of their unworthiness, a conviction arrived at by the rulers themselves, who, of course, had their reasons for so acquiescing in the general verdict. Now, though inequality is at the basis of all reasonable organization of collective life, without which specialization and hierarchy are unthinkable, the principle of equality, which is antagonistic to it, must also be satisfied, and this principle demands that inequality should be continuously justified by competence and merit. A true democracy must exact from its leaders an ever renewed proof of their capacity to lead. Unfortunately, our liberal-democratic leaders have not always been able to provide such a proof, and, what is worse, they have often thought that they would be excused from pro-

Liberal Democracy

ducing it by giving up their right and their duty to lead.

The consequences of this social phenomenon could hardly be exaggerated. We know that the axioms and postulates on which liberal democracies have lived for a century have been evolved with an almost complete disregard for the all-important rôle of hierarchy. To such natural tendencies the moral bankruptcy of leaders came to give a formidable impetus. Attacked both from below and from above, the pyramid of social and political authority crumbles down rapidly. This process of disintegration is one of the diseases which threatens to destroy altogether the liberal-democratic system in the nations which still remain faithful to it.

INVASION OF TECHNIQUE

Nowhere is political life more active than in democracies, and though, in theory, this should not be so, it is a matter of fact and of human nature that a touch of drama and even sometimes of sensation is indispensable to keep the people interested in politics. *The play is the thing.* Unfortunately for democratic institutions the problems of collective life become more and more boring and abstruse. Again in Hamlet's language, they are caviare to the general. The politicians themselves are unable to form an opinion without the aid of experts. No statesman dares move nowadays without a host of specialists who prompt him on what he ought to think and has to say. Let it, moreover, be considered

Ways and Practices

that the politician passes and the expert remains, that, to his technical knowledge, he thus adds the many and obvious advantages of continuity in office, and it will be realized that a modern democracy, by the sheer force of things, transfers to obscure and politically irresponsible experts the sovereignty which is supposed to reside in the people. This inevitable evolution contributes not a little to discrediting the higher levels of political hierarchy, and therefore, from the point of view of liberal democracies, must also be counted as a cause of disintegration.

But the invasion of technique is no less damaging to democracy in that it puts out of court the citizen himself. We have seen that the assumptions of theoretical democracy as to the competence, diligence, and sense of responsibility wherewith citizens study and decide problems of State are belied by facts, through the unwillingness of citizens to give time and effort to collective life; we now may add that, even if they were willing to give their time, they are becoming less and less able to make it yield any practical and useful results, through the growing complexity and technical difficulty of the problems to be examined. In one way the art of government is fast becoming a speciality beyond the capacity and competence of the ordinary citizen.

Simultaneously, and by a curious effect of compensation, the citizen gradually evicted by technique as an agent of government is more and more absorbed by technique as an object of government. The State, through the growing complication of collective life, meddles more and more with the activities of ordinary citizens, who thus tend to become mere pieces in an intricate official machinery. The citizen loses both ways: he has less control over the affairs of the State because they are so complicated that he can no longer master them; and he feels more control of the State over his own affairs because the State is so complicated that it must control everybody. It is obvious that these two lines of evolution combine again to weaken all belief in liberty and democracy, and, therefore, to disintegrate the liberal-democratic system.

THE INVASION OF ECONOMICS AND FINANCE

Yet, strong and deep as the influence of all these factors has been in the disintegration of liberal-democratic communities, it is doubtful whether all of them put together have produced so much havoc as the fatal twist inflicted on politics by the growing weight which economic and financial power bring to bear upon them. The discredit of democracy in the ranks of the people, the paradox of our times, is due above all to the gradual disillusionment which has invaded the popular soul at the sight of democratic institutions inevitably falling under the sway of the uncontrolled powers of industry and finance. This is no doubt the most serious problem of collective life, the one which demands the most exacting qualities of intellectual control for its right solution. It is considered in this chapter only from the point of view of its influence on the crisis of liberal democracies.

Ways and Practices

THE TYRANNY OF PRODUCERS

The tyranny of producers over the nation as a whole follows a clearly defined rhythm. As a direct consequence of ill-understood liberty, a medium of unlimited competition combined with the all too human tendency to greed, leads the employer, half willingly, half inevitably, to an unscrupulous exploitation of labour; this is the period of the early nineteenth century in England, a period through which other nations are still living in our day. The reaction against such a state of affairs brings forth trade unionism, which, in its turn, leads to the setting up of employers' associations. A civil strife follows in which the nation always loses, whichever of the two parties wins; at times the two industrial parties combine, and then it may be taken for certain that the alliance of the two brother-enemies of production will be made in most cases at the expense of the consumer.

This is a telegraphic sketch of the whole process. But, in its development, it goes through phases of the utmost importance for our present purpose. The employer, and in general the owner of the means of production, occupies a position of enormous political power in the State. This aspect of democratic life has been so often analysed that no time need be wasted here beyond that needed to put it on record. Rightly, in most cases, the working classes have jeered at a democracy which has prevented them from voting as their heart directed for fear of losing their daily bread. The situation appealed to them as an intolerable caricature of equality, while their precarious economic situation, which, through low salaries and unemployment, chained them to a particular district, appealed to them as an equally intolerable caricature of liberty. Such a background of disillusionment as to ideas, strengthened by the moral and physical suffering which poverty and insecurity are bound to entail, and leavened by the spiritual and intellectual revelation of the printed book, explains how the working classes have come to acquire a state of mind of permanent tacit revolt. What was the use of democracy?

It is easy to understand how in this state of mind a certain callousness towards the upper or possessing classes should have been extended to the whole nation. The fatal doctrine of class struggle acted in the same direction. Thus the worker came naturally to consider the strike as a political weapon, since his adversary, the employer, made a political weapon of industrial power. Now, in the mass of the nation this reiterated use of the strike for political purposes was bound to have disastrous effects. The moment has not yet come to discuss the legitimacy of strikes and lock-outs in civilized society, but we know enough to say, as a matter of mere common sense, that to declare a general strike in order to impose the views of part of the community on the whole of it is to lack sense of proportion altogether. It is evident that the doctrine which has been evolved with regard to strikes and lock-outs is but the result of the degeneration of liberal democracy, a manifestation of its weakness and of its tendency to capitulate before any show of force from whatever quarter it may come; if from employers, because of the State's incapacity to resist the economic power of capitalism; if from workers, because of a feeling of shame at refusing to the worker what is granted to the employer.

As a result of this dereliction of duty on the part of liberal-democratic leadership the nation becomes a kind of arena in which a continuous strife goes on between capital and labour on the industrial as well as on the political plane, without a single voice being raised to remind both combatants that neither of them is the nation; while the State is either powerlessly passive or wavering between subservience to the quiet powers of capital and weakness before the moral and industrial power of labour. The disorder to which this state of affairs drives, not merely the machinery of State, but the machinery of life, from international trade to the housewife's morning supply, wears out the democratic faith of the staunchest democrat and the belief in liberty of the most fanatical liberal.

The situation which has been evolved through misconceptions of principle and derelictions of duty on the part of governments is curious. Liberal democracies began under the aegis of economic liberty which forbade the State to intervene in economics. Once this preconception was well established, politics and economics went ahead in what one might have expected to be mutual ignorance; but while politics kept to the bargain, economics,

Liberal Democracy

more aware of what a bargain is, did not. And, therefore, while politics ignored economics, economics took a growing interest in politics. We know how, through the normal and abnormal exercise of economic power, political influence was gradually absorbed by employers and financiers at one end and by trade unions at the other. This evolution led to the lamentable fact that, while a relationship between politics and economics had not been studied on the basis of reason and from the point of view of the interest of the State, such a relationship nevertheless grew by haphazard and on the basis of a pull and push of influence, civil strife, corruption, lock-outs, strikes, and, in general, mental anarchy and political disorder.

The most striking symptom of this state of affairs is unemployment. Born for the most part of the unplanned—perhaps inevitably unplanned—development of production, grown more acute and more frequent owing to the unlimited and unregulated power to create money which banks enjoy, unemployment is treated *simultaneously*

(a) As a nuisance;
(b) As an occasion for charity;
(c) As an economic phenomenon to be solved by economic science;
(d) As a political tool for the opposition (whether they be capitalist or labour);
(e) As the "just" claim of labour against a society "which must guarantee to every citizen the right to work."

And, as a result of these diverse and incoherent considerations, the public purse is opened and there leaks out the dole.

Now the dole is a sore in the body politic. It breeds moral and political corruption. It is as bad for the individual as for society. For it deprives the individual of his self-respect and accustoms him to an unhealthy economic life; and, as for society, let alone the mere financial consequences which are disastrous, the dole amounts to a subsidy granted by parliament to those who elect it. Unemployment is one of the most difficult problems of the present anarchical form of our collective life. The dole is the worst possible remedy for it, short of starvation.

POWER OF FINANCE

As if so many troubles did not suffice, the people of liberal democracies grow daily more and more aware of the extent to which finance pulls the strings of all the puppets of the show, the State, the workers, and even the employers. The absorption of all powers by the dispensers of credit is one of the most fantastic phenomena of contemporary life. As it develops in depth and not in surface, its importance is hardly realized even by those who have given it some attention. In a sense it is but the logical development of the economic or material age. All societies must live on a faith, and it is but natural that our society should rest on something as akin to faith as credit (from *credere*, to believe, as every schoolboy is supposed to know). Faith is a spiritual athlete carrying what conviction would groan and collapse under. Credit, a materialistic descendant of Faith, is also fairly athletic, for it carries the belief in the existence of formidable sums of money which no one ever saw nor is likely to see. Here is Professor Soddy's analysis of this all-important mystery of our economic religion:

> Before the war it was considered "safe" for the banker to keep some £15 per £100 of cash against deposits. That is, for every £100 deposited £15 of cash sufficed for the small cash demands, most of the depositors' purchasing power being exercised by cheque. We may take this 15 per cent for purpose of illustration only. It is doubtful if as much has been necessary for a very long time.
>
> Now the whole secret of the system is contained in the fact that when a bank creates a loan and lends £100 to a borrower, to do so it need only have £15 of its depositors' money, or whatever the "safe" ratio may be.
>
> Thus, dealing throughout with averages, against the original depositor of £100, £15 of legal tender must be kept in the till, leaving £85 available to be lent to a borrower. It is true this borrower might demand it in cash, but, on the average for him no less than for the original depositor, only 15 per cent of cash, or £12 15s., is necessary, leaving £72 5s. free to be lent to a second borrower. Of this 15 per cent, or £10 17s., again suffices to be retained, leaving £61 8s. available to be lent to a third borrower. So it goes on until each £100 of original cash becomes a total of £666 13s. 4d. Of this £100 are due to the depositor and £566 13s. 4d. is owing to the bank from the borrowers.

Ways and Practices

The borrowers have to deposit with the bank acceptable collateral securities, which, if they default, the bank can sell, or try to sell, to recoup itself. But such securities are usually not sold. The bank charges interest upon the fictitious loan. At a modest 5 per cent bank rate the interest on £566 13s. 4d. is £28 6s. 8d. per year, which is, it must be admitted, not a bad return on £100 which the original "depositor" *has not lent.*

If the truth were known it would probably be found that this estimate is altogether too modest.[1] At least since, if not before, the war the figures suggest rather a 7 per cent "safe" limit than 15 per cent. On this basis a client depositing £100 of cash in current account enables the bank to loan £1,330, which at 5 per cent brings in £66 10s. 9d. per annum.[2]

It is obvious that, through the operation of this system, the banks have attained two aims fatal both to democracy and to liberty: they have all but evicted the State from its position as the only dispenser of money; and they have all but evicted the industrialist from his position as the manager and controller of industry, that is to say, from his position as promoter or *entrepreneur,* which was, by the way, his classical justification for the exorbitant privileges which he claims in the economy of the nation. The world is nowadays governed by the central banks, and the central banks, theoretically

---

[1] Hugo Bilgram (*Journal of Political Economy*, xxix, November 1921) takes the total of cash reserves held by deposit and reserve banks in the United States as not less than 8 per cent of the total deposit currency, and of this 40 per cent must be gold.

[2] *Wealth, Virtual Wealth, and Debt,* by Professor Frederick Soddy. London: George Allen and Unwin Ltd.

the mothers or aunts of the private banks, are, in fact, their servants and wet nurses. An entirely irresponsible power has arisen which neither Plato nor Montesquieu had thought of, which controls the wealth and in general the life of nations far more efficiently than any monarch or dictator ever did—the banker. The only limit to his power is in the objective complications of the material he handles. But if, through a combination of his personal competence and of favourable circumstances, he is able to play on the keyboard of money and prices without striking too many false notes, there is no limit to what the banker can do. Neither King nor Parliament has power over him. Democracy is forgotten and liberty loses its meaning.

Not a word in all this about his indirect and illegitimate material influence over political life. Finance might be—it sometimes is—above all suspicion of ingratiating itself with public men by means of directorships, large fees, loans without interest, credit facilities for their more or less disinterested friends; of influencing newspapers, of buying votes, of subscribing to election expenses or political propaganda; it might be as white as snow with regard to any political use of its money—the fact would remain that, through the practically unlimited power to create money which it has evolved, finance has been one of the most active causes of the disintegration of the liberal-democratic State and of the decadence of the liberal-democratic faith.

Ways and Practices

INTERNATIONALIZATION OF POWER

The weakness of government action has always been one of the inherent characteristics of liberal democracies. Every fact or circumstance which tends to increase such weakness, even if it be not directly connected with liberal-democratic principles or practices, is bound, by a kind of contamination, to contribute to the discredit of liberal democracies. Now, our age has evolved a circumstance of its own which has undermined government power to a considerable extent. The rapid growth of international solidarity—not, be it noted, in the sphere of thought and of emotions, in which it lingers sadly behind what it should be, but in the sphere of facts and interests, in which mechanical inventions and the evolution by which they have been determined have rushed ahead—has gradually reduced the area of national life on which the fiat of the national government is still the only law. A growing number of facts of daily occurrence are subject to the gravitation of foreign events. A coal strike in England may save a negotiation between Germany and Poland for a commercial treaty. A protectionist decree of the Spanish Government may cause hunger in the Welsh coal areas. A threat of war in the Far East may save American cotton farmers from ruin. This chaining together of national events with events in other nations reduces the power of governments while it increases the aggregate power of finance, which exerts itself precisely in the subtle and mobile atmosphere of interconnected national markets. Many good observers believe that the 1929 crash which started our present crisis was determined by the policy stubbornly pursued by the unaided and unfettered brain and conscience of the then Governor of the Federal Reserve Bank, whose power of life and death (bread and hunger) over men far exceeded those of any Tsar. But apart from the increase of power which the internationalization of economic life has brought to some men or institutions, the reduction of the efficiency and authority of governments which it implies has no doubt contributed to discredit the liberal-democratic system. For reasons which cannot be analysed here, this crisis, though purely international, manifests itself in nationalistic tendencies, such as that towards excessive protection and to autarchy. These tendencies, in their turn, increase the crisis, and, by the ill-humour thus fostered, a further danger for liberal-democratic systems develops in our present world.

THE PRESS

Nothing but the gradual character of the evolution which has brought the Press to the position which it occupies in contemporary society can explain the amazing fact that the most important organ of public life should be left to the vagaries and hazards of private ownership. Yet an explanation is not a justification. What should we think of a nation which allowed its Parliament to be appointed by a few private individuals and run for profit? Yet the Press, which, in political life, is nearly as important as, and sometimes more important than, Parliament, is entirely in the hands of a few individuals and is run for profit. If an Irish bull be permitted, it might be said that once one thinks about it it becomes unthinkable. No doubt the power of the Press may be exaggerated. No doubt cases have been seen in all nations when elections have turned out exactly contrary to the opinions advocated by the most powerful organs of the Press. But the minimum that can be said against the present system is formidable enough, and would at any rate comprise the following items:

1. The present system subordinates the public interest—good and true information—to the private interest of the firm. This means
    (a) That any other private interest strong enough to make it worth while has a good chance to exercise a censorship of its own on views and news;
    (b) That a newspaper may find it to its interest, and it often does, to appeal to the lower passions of its readers.
2. It places a few men, chosen on purely artificial grounds, in key positions as regards the forming of public opinion. Thus, merely because they happen to possess so many shares in a newspaper, a handful of men mould public opinion more effectively than others. At least the key positions of finance (Governorships of Central Banks, for instance) are not usually attained without competence.

But a man may fancy to take up the newspaper line as he might take up shoe-making or underwear.
3. It enables men to keep from the public things which ought to be known; from the point of view of the deformation of facts the silence of newspapers is far more important than their news.
4. It gives to a few men a weapon of untold power over politicians, since a newspaper can make or mar many a political career.

This is not yet the moment to suggest how these evils may be remedied, if indeed a remedy can be found for them. But, in an inventory of the ways and practices of liberal democracies, the gradual absorption of public power by the Press at the expense of the organs constitutionally organized had to be mentioned. There are countries in which organizations of news and publicity based on the Press have more power than governments and parliaments, and in all liberal democracies the Press is a substantially constitutional problem which would not have remained beyond the boundaries of the Constitution if it had not been made taboo precisely because of the power of the Press and of the fear it puts in the hearts of politicians.

In recent years the problem has become further complicated by the exceptional development of telegraphic agencies. States of powerful countries have stimulated the creation and growth of these agencies which act directly or indirectly as agents

Ways and Practices

of propaganda for the nations concerned. The newspapers subscribe to them and receive in exchange a generous current of telegrams with the latest news carefully filtered, and also with the latest declarations, hardly disguised, of the official in charge of propaganda in the nation from which the money comes. But such official, semi-official, or officious declarations, as well as the discreetly graded indiscretions which are "released" now and then, are not the most important forms of national propaganda. The subtlest and most penetrating of the ways in which this new art is carried out is the colouring of news. The existence of these vast and powerful organizations for the supply of news is one of the most difficult aspects of the thorny problem of the Press which has thus been transferred from the national to the international plane.

DEGENERATION OF POLITICAL INSTITUTIONS

It would be strange, indeed, if the combined effect of all these aberrations, confusions, and malpractices did not tell on the actual working of political institutions. And of course it does. Perhaps the most important of the distortions thus inflicted on the liberal-democratic system by the shortcomings of human nature is the tendency to transform parliamentary representatives into the mandatory agents of the most influential of the local interests in the representative's electoral district. No one with any experience of public affairs can have failed to observe the importance of this real cancer of collective life, particularly acute in liberal democracies. The representative must not only adjust his opinions and the level of his political thought to the opinions and to the political level of his electors—which is bad enough in most cases—but, what is even much worse, he must open a shop, office, or agency, to listen to the claims, justified or unjustified, of his electors. The unhappy representative spends his time, not as he ought to do and theoretically does, studying the general problems of the nation and what one might call the general local problems, but coming and going from government department to government department, placing a schoolmaster here and a postman there, and obtaining protective rights for the goods of this or that powerful subscriber to his electoral funds. The disease is known and has been diagnosed as classical in all books of political medicine or quackery. It is, unfortunately, all too frequent, and it afflicts equally presidential countries, such as the United States of America, and parliamentary countries, such as France.

There are other troubles of liberal democracies which may be observed to afflict with unequal vigour presidential and parliamentary systems. Presidential systems tend to over-emphasize the personality of the President. Situations of the utmost complexity—and all are so nowadays—the development of which for better or for worse is far less predictable than the weather, serve notwithstanding as the basis for the making or marring of political fortunes. A President is re-elected for having conferred prosperity as a boon to the country, and he

Ways and Practices

is unseated for having produced an economic crisis, which amounts to voting for or against a man according to whether during his time of office the weather was wet or dry. The result of this personalization of politics is that all events are conceived, prepared, announced, commented upon, and presented from the point of view not of efficiency but of effect. The gravest questions of international or national life are, more often than not, treated as jumping boards for a political sensation which, as the phrase goes, is *sprung* upon the world in order to keep its mouth gaping and its eyes round with admiration for the Great Man—the while pressmen feverishly swarm to the telegraph room and pour out streams of superlatives as adequate to the genuine situation as are the exultations of the green lover to the battered charms of the experienced lady whom he adores. Whoever has witnessed this kind of tragi-comedy carries in his memory abundant food for thought on liberal-democratic institutions.

Nor is the parliamentary system better calculated to ensure a sound working of the Executive. The President in a presidential system seeks the basis for his policy in direct touch with the mass. Hence the Big Man psychology. The cabinet in a parliamentary system depends entirely on its parliamentary majority. Hence either disastrous cascades of ministries or a policy of hesitation and compromise due to a mixture of politics and arithmetic. Now an Executive must possess two indispensable qualities: it must know what it wants, and it must live long enough to do it. Political arithmetic, the dosage of

Liberal Democracy

parties and mutual jealousies prevent cabinets from formulating too clearly what they want, so that parliamentary governments hardly ever know what they do want; and as for living long enough to perform it, everyone knows that a parliamentary cabinet is as short-lived as happiness, inspiration, or innocence—three things, by the way, hardly ever found in politics, liberal or otherwise.

There is one other point, a most delicate one, which must be mentioned, for it is fundamental. Politics cost money. Parties need a budget; the public man must live and his family also. Nothing more obscure and complicated than the finance of politics. Something was said on the matter when discussing the politics of finance. The budgets of extreme parties are easy to explain. Big landed property and big capital provide the funds needed to keep the political front well manned. Socialist parties thrive on the income provided by the unions. But it is precisely the middle parties, i.e. those which incarnate the liberal-democratic ideas, the backbone, therefore, of liberal democracies, whose finances are the most precarious and, therefore, the most exposed to receive in their ranks individual scouts, freebooters, adventurers, or simply well-meaning men whose conscience has become elastic under the pressure of necessity and the disillusion of years. This is by no means to suggest that liberal-democratic parties are less honest than the extreme ones, but it cannot be doubted that the liberal-democratic system, precisely because it lays less stress than others on group discipline and more stress than others on individual freedom, is a more favourable medium for the development of political corruption, or, at least, of political loose ways. As a grave corollary of this situation, a certain shrinking from political life may be observed in many a liberal-democratic country among the most scrupulous and clean-living citizens, those precisely whose active co-operation should be most useful. The effect of this tendency, combined with that which we have already observed to compete downwards for votes, acts as an inverted selection, or, in Darwinian terms, the medium being bad, the survival of the fittest drives the best citizens to political destruction.

CONCLUSION

We have now come to the end of our review of actual political life in liberal democracies. Our task had for its object to define, as best we could, the evils and perils we must guard against if we wish, as of course we do, to retain our faith and to carry on, in actual collective life, the principles of true liberal democracy. As we look back on the long list of deformations, confusions, and vices which this system has evolved, we are impressed but we are not downcast. We do not feel ready to give up our principles, but we do believe they need re-thinking. We do not want to give up the forms of public life and government which they have inspired, but we do believe that they want reshaping. The world is drawn to dictatorships and to totalitarian States, guessing in them an experiment worth trying; meanwhile it is drawn away from democracy because it fears democracies are bigoted and unable to shed their slough. Let us try to suggest new experiments in democracy and liberty. But, in order to do so, let us keep our minds open and not cry sacrilege whenever we come to changes from which tradition may shrink, but which reason may recommend.

Part II
Unanimous Organic Democracy

CHAPTER III

The Principles of Unanimous Organic Democracy

THAT THE STATE HAS NO FINALITY

IN all things the end in view must be considered. Much as we may wish to avoid theoretical disquisitions, it is impossible to lay down a satisfactory scheme of collective life without being clear first as to what collective life is for. True, it is there and it need not be justified. But what is needed is not the justification of the fact of collective life, but an agreement as to its purpose and its finality without which nothing can be said as to the order of importance of the elements which compose it. The point has sprung to the first rank of our preoccupations, for of recent years the old doctrine which subordinates the individual to the State has gained new strength and dominates unchallenged in a few nations by no means unimportant. It is therefore necessary to discuss afresh this old controversy in order to build the rest of our work on solid ground.

Our opinion on this point is clear, so clear that, having expressed it once, all we can do is to restate it in exactly the same terms:

Human beings are the only real and tangible entities, the only creatures which really do exist and in whom all spirits and tendencies are manifested. Individual man is the home of liberty, of authority, of anarchy, of dictatorship, of order, of equilibrium, of the health of the State; and as for the nation, where does it exist if not in the hearts of its citizens, i.e. separately and completely felt in the heart of every one of the flesh-and-blood citizens who compose it?

It is not merely that the individual is king, but that he is the only thing there is. There is nothing but individuals, so much so that when from the heights of theoretical discussions we come down to the practical applications of the principles adopted, whatever they may be, we find it all amounts to relations of power between the individual-who-governs and the individual-who-is-governed, so that authoritarian governments differ from liberal governments in that under the former the individual-who-governs has more liberty, or in other words that, in the last resort, authority means liberty of the individual-who-governs.

It is true that these individuals would be less themselves, that they would live a far more elementary and vegetating life were there not institutions to insert them, so to speak, within an ensemble which constitutes a kind of social tissue. But the organic image, which was necessary to correct the mechanical errors of the nineteenth century, is dangerous in that it reduces the individual to the rank of a cell of the body, social or national, which therefore becomes the supreme end to which the individual is but the means. No, one thousand times no. The supreme end is the individual, and collective institutions should have no more hold over him than is needed for his own individual development.[1]

[1] Extract from a speech delivered at the University of Paris for the opening of the course of the Centre d'Études de la Revolution Française of the Faculty of Letters of the University. November 25, 1933.

The Principles

This unique position of the individual is not sufficiently taken into account when discussing political affairs. The principle laid down by Kant remains unchallenged, if it is fairly, i.e. adequately, interpreted. Man *is* an end in himself, for the simple reason that there is nothing else that can be an end. It is sometimes argued that the ends in themselves are the values: Truth, Beauty, Goodness. But these values are but forms of thought: of whose thought? Of the only being we know who can think: man. There is nothing outside of man. It is only through him and in him that Truth, Beauty, and Goodness have any sense; only by him that they can be served or betrayed. It is only in man that the spirit manifests itself. The arts, science, and philosophy, the art of government, civilization, all things exist in so far as they are created and consumed by men. The individual has therefore this title to finality, that he is the only claimant to finality there is. Other claims have been made—the values, the State —but they are the creations of man, and their claims are creations of man also.

The "State," moreover: what State? It is evident that no man ever lived in mental and physical isolation; that therefore a community of some sort is inseparable from man; that, on close observation, the individual appears much less distinct from his environment than his clearly outlined bodily frontiers and his mobility might lead to suppose; that, in short, the individual is a cell of a social tissue. Without a milieu with which he establishes a continuous set of actions and reactions the individual is,

Unanimous Organic Democracy

in fact, unthinkable. Robinson Crusoe himself was full of memories and hopes of his normal milieu. He was not an absolutely isolated man. Not even the anchorites of Tibet, who bury themselves alive, succeed in cutting themselves off entirely from the world; they carry with them into their voluntary tomb a religious culture and a set of memories which they owe to their previous phase of life within the community.

But while some sort of a community and, therefore, of a State is inseparable from the idea of the individual, nothing in the mind requires that this community or State should be precisely the national one. From the point of view of the deepest human necessities of the individual, the national State is not indispensable. The community, whatever its political basis, provides a framework for the individual's experience, a setting for his creative powers, an absorber of his energy, and a store of traditions and materials for life. From this point of view the individual and society stand in a relation similar to that between the pianist and the piano. The individual plays on the social keyboard. It is evident that the relationship will be the richer, and the individual life in question, all other factors on his side being equal, will be richer, in communities presenting a wider and a more complex keyboard. It is here and only here that the national element in the State takes on a specific importance. Till this moment the reasoning could apply to any community. Most individuals, moreover, can be easily "explained" by their village. But the background,

The Principles

the connotations, the language (mental and physical), the conventions, the culture of the community are considerably developed and enriched when strong States succeed in maintaining an organic society for a sufficient length of time. Historical continuity is the basis of culture. Culture is the collective basis of individual worth. Thus the national State appears, not as an indispensable but as an all-important element in the life of the individual.

Has this reasoning led us to imply or suggest that the State has a finality of its own? If, as we do in these pages, we mean by finality the specific quality of being an end in itself, we have to deny finality to the State since we have granted it to the individual. What is a State? It is a complex of institutions more or less harmoniously connected in theory and in practice, more or less stable, which embodies the collective traditions and administers the collective interests gathered in the course of history by a group of men on a given territory, when, for reasons also historical and involving therefore an element of chance, there exists between them a minimum of solidarity. This feeling of solidarity—in which may be discerned animal elements of consanguinity, geographical and climatic elements, sociological elements grown of habit, emotional elements due in part to common remembrances, intellectual elements in which a strong proportion of self-suggestion may be observed—is the root of the feeling of nationality. The process through which nationality is thus evolved owes much to the potent and unpredictable element in life.

Unanimous Organic Democracy

The result is so complex and so changing that, for instance, it would be difficult for the most sagacious psychologist to find much in common between the dukes and earls of contemporary English aristocracy, so urbane, so courteous and disciplined, and the half savages who bore their names and whom we find swearing, breaking their word, and soaking in blood and crime in the pages of Shakespeare's histories. It is difficult to see how entities so fluid and so subject to vicissitudes as nations can be endowed with finality at all. The humblest citizen of the humblest nation has finality; the proudest empire on earth has not. A man in whatever station he lives has in him that before which all other men must stand with respect: an unmovable destiny, a destiny the background of which, for all the most cocksure of us know, may go far beyond the limits of this life and rise far above the giddiest heights our mortal eyes can behold. The proudest empire on this earth is at best a historical instrument, roughly hewn by genius and brutality, slowly polished by talent and success, used for an age, discarded in the process of time, and finally buried away in the museums of history.

Of all the products which human humbug has elaborated, none more solemn, dangerous, and empty than the "historical missions" which have at one time or another been attributed to certain nations by those who write history as the Lord's private secretaries. We know that Spain had once the mission to save Europe from the infidel (who, by the way, at the time was far more civilized than the

The Principles

European), and later on that of opening up America to a Christianity which Europe had not and has not yet mastered, and if any doubt it let him come and see; we know that Napoleonic France had for her mission to sow the seeds of the French Revolution in the soil of Europe, soaked in blood for the purpose; we know that Great Britain has for its mission to carry the white man's burden, preferably on the shoulders of the coloured man; we know that the Union of Socialist Sovietist Republics has for its mission to raise the proletariat of the world from the slavery of capitalistic liberty to the liberty of communistic slavery. There are yet two or three more missions brewing: they can be located by observing the danger-signs of coming wars.

It will be noticed, moreover, that most "missions" are discovered *a posteriori*. It is only after a handful of free adventurers have tried and succeeded in getting a footing on the new ground, and when a host of more cautious and business-like settlers have come behind them, that a kind of historical blessing is poured over the adventure by a few solemn stay-at-homers. And then the mission appears.

It is all humbug and nonsense. Nations have no "missions." Nations cannot be said to exist at all to the extent of being entitled to claim a finality over and above that of the men who compose them. In fact, no nation ever claimed anything, because nations do not speak. It is men who speak for them. And the men who take upon themselves to speak on behalf of the nation may be expected to emit more humbug than their fair share if only because

Unanimous Organic Democracy

no normal person would care, unprovoked, to become the mouthpiece of so elusive, so complex, and so unpredictable a fact as a nation.

There is one way of looking at this matter which settles it once for all. If nations had such a claim to finality that citizens were reduced to the rank of their subjects, and the lives of the men who compose them had to be regulated only from the point of view of the nation's life, such men would thereby undergo a curtailment of their manhood. For *man*, I take it, is a higher, wider, deeper concept than *Englishman, Frenchman, American, Russian*. Nationalism is so dangerous as a mental disease precisely because it reduces the spiritual status of man. For my part, I shall never forget that most dramatic moment in the life of Captain Scott, his cool facing of certain death in the pure white Southern solitude; he was a believer; he was facing his Maker; and yet this man, brave and calm, did not write down: "I die like a man," but "I die like an Englishman." With all respect, with all admiration for the great nation and for her great son, what a come-down!

Nations, precisely because they divide men, can be no more than formal and instrumental. Any doctrine which attributes to them essence and finality can be founded neither on a religious, nor on a humanistic, view of life. All truly religious leaders, and all true humanists, must agree on this ground. There is no more dangerous heresy, and certainly none which stands as a heresy against a wider range of human thought and belief, than that which puts nation above man.

The Principles

THAT THE CITIZEN IS FOR THE STATE AND THE STATE IS FOR MAN

Once the claim of the State to finality has been disposed of, the relationship between the State and the individual can be studied, starting, of course, at the individual end. But this study requires yet another somewhat theoretical preliminary discussion. This individual, whose pre-eminent right to consideration we have (or think we have) established, what is he after, or as the Scottish catechism puts it with a truly Scottish sense of values: "What is man's chief end?" In the sixteenth century the answer would have been: "To save his soul by serving God." In the twentieth century it is more likely to be: "To seek happiness by all legitimate means." Now this answer will not do, because happiness is the most elusive and changeable of experiences. In the last resort happiness is the pleasure felt by the human being when his powers are absorbed by the milieu so exactly that there results a state of equilibrium. All in Nature, physical and moral, is performed in and by equilibrium. If the engine of a car is running without effecting any work, it gets hot and it ends in self-destruction, or at least is put out of order; if the resistance of weight and gradient is stronger than the engine, the engine is brought to a standstill; the normal working of the engine consists precisely in the equilibrium between its power and the resistance offered it by the outer world. Similarly, normal life in a human being consists in an adequate equilibrium between his physical, mental, and spiritual powers and the consumption of them which the world is able to make. The body's balance of food and hunger, love and libido, outgoing heat and atmospheric temperature, provide the basis of health necessary to happiness; over and above this basis man has in him will-power, talent, and vision in qualities and quantities the combination of which varies *ad infinitum*. His quest for happiness consists in his instinctive, intuitive, and conscious efforts to find a balance between such powers and the personal, social, business, and political relations which may absorb them exactly.

Thus defined, happiness obviously appears as an extremely precarious state, for it is most difficult to attain and most easy to lose. Difficult to attain because the equilibrium sought is the sum total of a large amount of component equilibria, since the loss of balance in any one of the planes in which it must be sought destroys happiness; thus, for instance, a man in love-equilibrium, that is to say, loving and loved, will not be happy if he suffers from hunger or if, being an ambitious and able man, he finds himself idle in exile. As for the instability of happiness, it is the obvious corollary of its complexity, for even if a man is fortunate enough to attain the numerous conditions of equilibrium needed for happiness, it is only natural that he who has so many things should lose at least one, and the lack of that one is enough, as we know, to destroy the effect of all the remaining possessions. Moreover, man's nature seems to be incompatible with happiness, since a relatively short

The Principles

duration of it withers the bloom of pleasure, which soon degenerates into boredom.

That the quest for happiness cannot be man's end in life is clear from this analysis, for it would lead to a fatal consequence, to wit, that since happiness cannot be attained unless all the powers of man are absorbed by the milieu, the safest road to happiness is to keep man down to a minimum of powers, i.e. to keep him undeveloped. The ephemeral character of happiness is a further inducement to believe that it is not man's aim but rather man's lure, and that, just as love is the lure whereby Nature uses man for her purpose in the service of the species, so happiness is the lure whereby Nature uses man in the service of the individual, that is, of man himself. Man's aim in life, therefore, would be, not happiness, but experience.

Experience is an essential part in the life of man, so essential indeed that human life is hardly conceivable without it. Experience is but life consciously and directly appraised by man from within. We find then that it is impossible to separate in practice the individual from the community, and that, as was to be expected, they are indissolubly connected by a relation which may be described as polar. What Nature gives us is a synthetical fact: the individual-in-society. We call *individual* one of the poles of this living fact; we call *society* the other. When we say *society*, we imply the existence of the individuals which it contains; when we say *individual*, we refer to man precisely as a member of the society. This polarity between the two ideas and the indissoluble

Unanimous Organic Democracy

connection of which it is the expression should be the guide to all thought on collective life and on all the ideas, such as liberty, equality, democracy, law, which collective life suggests.

We are now in possession of two fundamental thoughts on which to erect the rest of our construction: the first is that finality is an attribute of the individual and not of the State; the second is that the individual cannot be understood without a community which, for practical purposes and as a first approximation, we may take to be the State—a community to which he is connected by a polar relationship. From these premises two conclusions follow: the first is that the State can justify itself only as a servant of the citizens that compose it, a minister to their wants, a setting for their activities, an absorber of their energies, a guardian and an administrator of their several rights, a defender of their homes, and a promoter of their collective and individual culture. The second is that the State is entitled to curtail all non-essential liberties to the extent which may be necessary for its own constitution, preservation, and working. It is evident that no conflict can exist, at any rate in theory, between these two conclusions—the two conditions which the modern State must fulfil: whatever the complications which their fulfilment may produce in practice and whatever conflicts the inexperience and the imperfections of man may graft on such complications, the finality of an individual as a man and his subservience to the State as a citizen are perfectly compatible: for the State serves man in the realm of aims and values and is served by him in the realm of means and functions, or in one word: *the citizen is for the State and the State for man.*

The error of dictatorships and that which makes them inacceptable to free minds is that they have failed to see the second storey which the State must possess. The first storey, the functional State, is, with reservations, acceptable in principle, but only on condition that on this first plant of efficiency, work, function, and authority there rises the really essential plant of aims, the plant for which the other one exists and without which it is worthless; now, in this second storey of aims and values, liberty is the rule and man reigns as the master of his own thoughts and destinies.

LIBERTY AND AUTHORITY

Bearing in mind, then, the polar relation between the individual and society, we may now venture on an examination of the idea of liberty. We know that this idea is not for us an abstract quality which we might perhaps describe as a theological or metaphysical attribute of man. No. We mean to discuss, under the term of liberty, the ambit of unfettered movements of the individual in society. It is therefore in its essence a relative idea. It is not the theoretical stronghold from which man, absolute king of his volitions, gives away of his own accord to society such pieces of his self-government as he thinks fit. The principle of polarity which we have accepted leads us to suspect that liberty is the individual end of a force which must have as a counterpart a social end. This social counterpart of liberty is authority.

Thus the polarity individual-society is translated in the realm of tendencies or forces into the polarity liberty-authority. *Order* may be defined as the stable equilibrium between liberty and authority. If liberty prevails over authority, society falls into anarchy; if authority prevails over liberty, the individual falls into slavery. The position of equilibrium varies with the average psychological requirements of the individuals which compose the society and of the society itself. Thus under the same permanent psychological characteristics, a society in time of war or in any other emergency will require and attain a line of equilibrium nearer to the authoritarian pole than in time of peace and of general prosperity; which is but natural, because in times of stress society has more to do and the individual has a smaller margin for his personal activities; while in times of prosperity and of peace the individual feels his personal powers increase, and therefore requires a wider sphere for his activities.

Authors on political subjects, still under the influence of the relation which attaches their science to the science of morals, are wont to represent order as a blessing which nations can attain if they observe certain rules, and particularly if they keep a wise balance between liberty and authority. But the fact would appear to be the very reverse. Order does not result from achieving an adequate balance between liberty and authority; this adequate balance

The Principles

between liberty and authority results from the natural virtue of order which people possess when they do possess it. For (here again we meet with ever-present man) this balance between liberty and authority can only be realized in the individual. A society enjoys order if and when a sufficient number of its citizens achieve the balance of liberty and authority in their minds. When such a number of socially balanced people does not exist, a society cannot know a peaceful life. Three possibilities may arise:

(1) An excessive number of citizens fail to reach an adequate balance through an excess of individualistic tendencies, or, what amounts to the same, through an insufficient appraisal of the value of authority: the State then lives in permanent anarchy;

(2) A division sets in between two parts of the nation; the first is authoritarian, the second libertarian: the country then lives under constant threats of disorder and undergoes frequent crises of anarchy; for if the authoritarians are in command, they are temperamentally unable to absorb and organize the libertarians into civil life; while if the libertarians win, they are either unable to organize the State or else, through an all too frequent and natural paradox of human character, they become authoritarian on tasting power and reduce the nation to a thraldom which the other party is sure to resent;

(3) The majority of the citizens may fail to reach order through an excessive sense of authority, and this leads, not to order in the State, but to quiescence which, through lack of spontaneity in the obedience

obtained, is but a prelude to either revolt or degeneration.

Nothing in all this prejudges what liberty and authority should be, or what should be their relative values and their respective limits. So far we have been dealing with these two antagonistic tendencies as we might have discussed the mechanical relations between the two forces of cohesion and dispersion which physicists discriminate in physical bodies. The body politic has also its molecules, men, its force of cohesion, authority, and its force of dispersion, individual liberty. And so that the parallel may be complete, there are political bodies or communities in which authority or cohesion is stronger than liberty or dispersion, and thus they may be compared to solids; others in which liberty prevails over authority, and thus they resemble gases; while there is a middle or balanced type which may be likened to the liquids of physics, in which cohesion and dispersion, authority and liberty are even. And again, so that our comparison may accompany us all the way and give us assurance to think along the same line, these different states of political communities further resemble the states of matter in that they depend on circumstances; just as in physics heat makes solids pass into liquids and liquids into gases, historical circumstances may solidify the most undisciplined nation into an authoritarian State, only to leave it free to fall back again to its normal ways when the circumstances which had determined the change have passed.

These disquisitions are by no means set down

merely as curious or ingenious illustrations; they aim at conveying the relative and movable character of the ideas of liberty and authority which, handled by theoretical and legalistic minds, may have acquired a somewhat rigid and dogmatic aspect. We should envisage liberty not as a goddess, not as a figure of law, not as an abstract idea to be represented by a stone or bronze lady with a torch of the same material emitting dark radiations of nothingness into the void; but as a living tendency, fluid, undetermined, unharnessed, and unshaped, waiting in our living soul to shoot off in a definite form, direction, and intensity whenever a concrete stimulus is forthcoming. We should visualize authority as the tendency antagonistic to liberty, not, again, an abstract notion straight out of a book, but an urge to action and power on the part of a particular man occupying a key position in the State, an urge inextricably mixed with his own tendency to liberty, which happens at the moment to be harnessed by circumstances to the repression of the liberty of others with a view to fitting them into a collective system. For, let us say it again, nothing exists outside individual man and, though the feeling of authority in a community results from the *composition* (in the mathematical sense of the word) of the urge towards authority in all the men of the community, its actual expression in the State takes place through the instrumentality of the particular man or men in office; it manifests itself therefore with the colour, tendency, and intensity which this individual man or these individual men give it out of their own concrete personalities, and participates in the vigour of these concrete personalities, which implies that it participates in the sense of liberty in these men.

Thus understood as tendencies alive and relative, in mutual co-operation and antagonism—in fact, as the two faces of the same medal, the two opposite tensions on the same string—liberty and authority may now be studied in relation to the end of individual life on the one hand and to the function and utility of the State on the other.

THE TWO CLAIMS OF LIBERTY

Let us recall here Montesquieu's definition of liberty: "Liberty is the right to do all that the laws allow, and if a citizen were able to do what they forbid there would be no liberty left, for the others would also have the same power." This was a great achievement in Montesquieu's time. Tyranny consists in ruining the life of lawful citizens. Citizens then were apt to consider as an ideal that they should be allowed to live within the law. But in thus formulating the very modest ideal of his contemporaries, Montesquieu does not help us very much in our task of defining liberty. For the problem we have to solve is precisely that of determining how much of our liberty the State is entitled to curtail by means of its laws. Now, if we define our liberty as the power left us by the laws of the State, we are in a vicious circle. Since we are trying to solve a political problem, the terms for its solution must come from outside of and from above politics.

The Principles

Montesquieu himself tried his hand at this in the paragraph immediately preceding that quoted above, for he says: "Political liberty does not consist in doing what one pleases. In a State, i.e. in a society in which there are laws, liberty can only consist in being able to do what one must will to do and in not being bound to do what one must not will to do." Or in other words attributed to Georges Clemenceau: "Liberty is the right to do one's duty." Now, this is either too elliptical or quite meaningless. For the point in liberty is not so much whether the individual is allowed to do his duty as whether he, or someone else, is to define what his duty is, and, what is infinitely more important, whether he is to do his duty spontaneously or under coercion; and finally—yes, what is not merely more important but the crux of the matter—whether he is to do his duty if he does not want to.

It is useless to mince words. Liberty does mean in the last resort the right to misbehave. Let us remember the conclusions at which we have already arrived: the aim of man is to find himself in experience. What experience is this which "the laws," i.e. other men, are to limit and dictate? No one can go to heaven if he is not free to go to hell. Under compulsion there is no goodness. Liberty measures the area of man's responsibilities, and therefore the liberty of man must be as wide as possible so that his responsibility is wide and his experience rich. Our first principle of practical politics will therefore be that liberty need not justify itself; what must be justified at every step is restriction of liberty. Of course, man's misbehaviour will meet its fate—if ethical on the plane of ethics, if legal on the plane of law. What we claim is by no means man's right to misbehave and get away with it, but his right not to be deprived of the experience of his freely chosen misbehaviour. This first title to liberty on the plane of ethical experience is the most sacred of all and that which the State is most bound to respect. The State has no right to enter the *Sancta Sanctorum* of individual conscience. The laws which are to be made by the State in its capacity of defender of the liberty of other citizens against the encroachment of any one citizen must be delicately poised so as not to smother those very liberties it sets out to defend. Legislation on matters of ethics and private life should be sparingly given forth.

There is in human activities a whole gamut of shades, starting from the purely individual, ethical and private, and leading up to the purely functional, social and public. The prima facie claim of the State to intervene in behaviour grows, of course, as our actions take on a more social and functional aspect; the prima facie claim of the individual to be left alone grows as actions penetrate further and further into the realm of privacy. It is impossible to draw the line between these two sets of action, for there is no line whatever to be drawn. Here, as in everything vital, the change-over is gradual, cases are all complex and original, and the unexpected is normal. This adds a further reason for considering the relations between liberty and authority as an equilibrium between moving tendencies rather than

The Principles

as an opposition of antagonistic rigid ideas. There is in man's life an intimate zone to which the State can have no access by nature. All a man thinks and feels without outward manifestation is man's own undisputed possession. Tyranny has no hold on that. It is therefore clear that the problem arises when actions begin, as indeed was obvious from the very beginning, since we are dealing with political problems and politics belongs to the realm of action. When therefore a claim is made by the individual to liberty of thought, what is really claimed is not the right to think as and what one pleases, which no one can deny to anybody, still less wring from anybody; but the right to communicate one's opinions and the right to act according to them. These two rights are of the utmost importance from the point of view of the individual, as we shall see they are from the point of view of society. For it is indispensable that the individual should include mental experience in his life's experience, and therefore the interchange of views with other men by word or writing is an essential condition which no State has normally the right to oppose. And as to the right to act in harmony with one's convictions, its importance is so obvious for man's experience that to state it is to prove it.

Similar arguments apply to the life of the passions. The State cannot prevent the emotional life of a man from taking the course prescribed by nature and destiny. But as the passions emerge on the plane of actions a prima facie case for State interference arises. We shall examine it when we deal with the social pole of the problem. Here, from the individual pole, we know that the higher interests of the individual are coincident with the maximum liberty and the richest experience which he can achieve. This does by no means imply that man is to do what he pleases, nor, as naïvely suggested by Montesquieu, that he is to be free to do his duty, but that he is to be allowed to carry the burden of his responsibilities alone. All communities have evolved from the depth of their history and psychology a set of unwritten laws which govern behaviour in all that concerns the intimate passions. Men must be left the liberty to obey or break these laws. Political laws, so far as we know, and with all reservations as to what the examination of the problem from the point of view of the State may suggest, should abstain from interfering.

The second claim of liberty rises out of the search for happiness, which as we know is the stimulus for experience. Happiness requires an adequate medium for absorbing the energies of man. The organization of the State should be so understood that, by the operation of individual liberty, every man finds his level and his medium. No doubt a super-socialistic republic, superbly governed by super-psychological bureaucrats, could, by the use of mathematically exact tests, adjust energies and talents in the State to perfection: yet, while such ideal machinery is being evolved, the best State from the point of view now considered will be that in which individual liberty can operate like the fluid freedom of liquids, enabling everyone to move up and down until he finds his level.

The Principles

INEQUALITY

It will be observed that this image brings into the debate the idea of inequality. Such a fact was to be expected. Only historical reasons too well known to be restated and the confusions which attach to simple and general words can explain that liberal democracies should have written on their banners Liberty *and* Equality, two ideas which seldom go together in actual life. Inequality is the inevitable consequence of liberty. Even if, by a thoroughly rapid and successful revolution, a society started off all its citizens scratch, the natural differences between them would suffice to separate them in the race; a minority would rush ahead; the majority would run in the middle; a minority would lag behind. Equality of results could only be achieved by discriminating against the more intelligent, the more active, the more efficient, all of which would be both unfair and disastrous, or by discriminating against the most unscrupulous, which of course might be done without harm.

Democracies suffer from a prejudice against inequality which wastes away much of their energy. Inequality cannot and must not be rubbed out of the surface of life. Needless to say, there is no question here of unjustified privileges granted by law or grabbed by power. Such things cannot be defended, but that the scheme of collective life cannot be conceived without inequality in fact, and that it is a good thing that it should be so, is obvious. Inequality starts at birth. Brothers born under the same roof and bred in the same home set off in different directions, rise to different heights, found families whose fortunes differ as profoundly as those of utter strangers. The initial unfairness of class is constantly being corrected precisely through the action of individual liberty, which brings out the incapacity of some men to maintain a social situation too high for them and therefore causes their downfall, and the capacity of other men to rise to higher positions than those in which they happen to be, and determines therefore a movement upwards in society. By means of this mechanism due to individual liberty there is, in society, a kind of mutual permeation whereby men of the manual classes pass into the bourgeoisie in rather stronger contingents than men in the middle classes fall down to the salaried layers. The classes themselves overlap, since nowadays in most countries the poorer ranks of the middle classes are much worse off than the richer ranks of labour. But even if such justifications did not come to comfort those who, from mental habit, object to inequality, inequality is a fact which nothing can correct, not even the strong hand of a communistic dictatorship. If a return to a comparison with physics be allowed, inequality is as essential in human societies as in all the aspects of life which physics describes to us. Whether in the play of waters and of solid materials on the surface of the earth, in the different levels of mountains, valleys, and plains, or in the actions of heat and electricity, all that moves, in one word, energy, is but a manifestation of differences of level. Suppress differences

The Principles

of level, and at once you deprive man of the mill, of hydroelectric power, of the steam engine, and of the electrical engine; further still, suppress differences of level, and there are no more hills, no sea, no rivers; the circulation of water, which is to the earth what the circulation of blood is to the human body, ceases and the planet becomes a sepulchre lost in the void. Differences of level in society are of no less importance. A society lives, thanks to the play of tensions formed within it, precisely by the differences of level which it contains. Without inequality, therefore, collective life would lose all its value as a field of experience. The web of life is made of these differences. Culture, art, love, history, would be the poorer without the inequalities of life, and the effort upwards, which is one of the most deeply rooted instincts in social man, would disappear in a society levelled to an average which would have to be perforce very modest.

Moreover, inequality implies at the lower end a danger limit—the much feared line of *necessity*—and necessity is an indispensable element both in collective and in individual life. This is a hard saying, and one which democracy does not like to hear. But the harm done to democracy by the lack of courage of its intellectual workers is incalculable. Necessity is to society and to the individual what gravity is to the physical world. The action of weight, the fact that all things, unless held up, fall as low as they can go, is so frequent a happening that we are apt to undervalue its immense importance. All material life is based on it, and though it seems a drag on life it is its most potent spring. Whoever doubts it, let him devote a few seconds of reflection to that most natural and humble phenomenon of mechanical life: that water, of its own, always seeks the lowest level. Similarly, the fact that man, unless he holds himself up with all his energy, will fall as low as he can go down to the line of want, is one of the most potent springs of collective life, and if it were removed the community would soon pay dearly and the individual himself would undergo a rapid decadence.

A State which sets out to abolish necessity emasculates its citizens. George Bernard Shaw, whom communists will not disavow, has strongly criticized the system whereby clever boys are selected from their tender age by a system of scholarships which conveys them comfortably to the top of their education and launches them forth in life totally undeveloped in character for lack of opportunities for effort. The brilliant Irishman may have let the fire of his criticism burn too hot: education without financial effort is the lot of 90 per cent of well-to-do students, and amongst them the proportion of individuals with a well-developed character is high. Nor, as will be seen in its proper place, is it suggested here that those who fall to the bottom of the ladder of inequality should be allowed to perish in starvation. What is put forward here on general lines of principle, to be elaborated into positive suggestions later on, is that necessity should have its recognized place in the scheme of collective life because, from the point of view of the individual (the point of view

The Principles

here considered), it is one of the most potent springs of experience. He is no sincere, or no consistent, advocate of liberty who does not acknowledge necessity as the reverse of the medal, for liberty means risk and risk may mean loss.

Inequality suggested itself to us while we were dealing with the second aspect of liberty, i.e. the scope of individual activity. It bears also a close relationship to liberty considered under a third point of view, what might be described as the elbow-room of function. This is, of course, the aspect of individual liberty in which its polarization with authority stands out most clearly. The individual as a member of the community has certain functions to fulfil. They imply certain powers or liberties. He must have them. They are functional liberties; they translate themselves into functional inequalities. But, on this plane, adjustment is relatively easy, and the balance between society and the individual is automatically attained since the individual here is acting as the representative of the State.

LIBERTY AND THE STATE

When from the point of view of the individual we pass to that of the State, the conclusions at which we have arrived will be found to agree with those we are about to formulate since, as we know by now, we shall be examining the same subject though from the other pole. The idea which from the social pole corresponds to liberty is authority. Now, under this concept, it is possible to discriminate several elements which may be examined under three heads: first, the latitude which the State must possess to act on the individual as trustee of the liberties of all other citizens; second, the latitude which the State is entitled to possess to ensure its own preservation and working; and finally, there is always within the authority of the State an element emanating from the tendency to individual liberty in the man who happens to incarnate the State at the time, and this element may often be in actual fact the most powerful of the three.

It is evident that in its first capacity the State cannot be a threat to the real interests of individual liberty, since under this head authority is but what mathematicians would describe as the *integral* of the liberty of all citizens. This is perhaps the moment to point out that individual liberty, which we saw as essential for the individual, is also essential for the State, or in other words that the State is most flourishing when it can secure the plane of equilibrium between liberty and authority, as near as possible to liberty. This is not a phrase, nor a hankering, nor an idealistic illusion; it is a fact which can be proved. For, under a regime of maximum liberty, the fluidity of the social medium is at its best, and citizens can most easily reach the rank and function which is most adequate to their capacity and social utility. Moreover, that liberty of thought which we proved to be indispensable for the individual happens also to be indispensable for the State. This may be shown both on political grounds and on grounds of culture. On political grounds, because a State must

The Principles

be governed according to a general scheme of ideas, what we might describe as a political philosophy or a political truth; now, political truth may be defined as the least inadequate relation between men's minds and their environments at any given time. This definition suggests at least two reasons why freedom of thought should be indispensable for the community: the first is that the attainment of this least inadequate relation must be sought at every moment and by a continuous adaptation, in other words, by a kind of continuous intellectual experience which in itself presupposes liberty, both for investigation and for the handing down of findings and results; the second reason is that we seek a truth and a knowledge which must be collective both in their object and in their subject; it is the community which must know, and what it must know is the community; therefore, without liberty of thought there can be no collective knowledge, and without collective knowledge there can be no community.

There is a further reason why liberty of thought is all-important from the collective point of view on political grounds. Two of the main functions of the community are an intelligent and informed criticism of the activities of the State and the selection of the State's leading staff. It is hardly necessary to insist on the importance of free thought for the adequate supply of critics as well as for their education, so that they can adequately fulfil their delicate functions and for the information which they need to that effect. A State without freedom of thought cannot be properly criticized, and is therefore doomed to degenerate through the natural corruptive effect of unfettered power. But freedom of thought is even more important in the formation of the leaders which every community must possess, for, without freedom of thought, there can be no enlightened public opinion, no stimulus to public life, no reflection on public affairs, no leaders.

This argument in favour of liberty of thought from the point of view of politics naturally leads to a consideration of its importance from the point of view of culture. Culture is the most important of the aims for which the State exists. We are thus led to examine the State in itself, not merely as the trustee of the liberty of all citizens, but as the vessel in which a certain form of collective life is contained with a minimum of continuity to enable it to produce a culture. But culture, again, is for us an essentially individual affair. It is only to be found in men or as a reflection of men. All the values which go to the making of culture are stored up by national continuity under the wing of the State. In this way men find it easier to acquire the first elements of information and, through education as well as through the moulding effect of home and town, to receive the impressions of moral, aesthetic, and social influences which are the beginnings of culture. To create and to maintain culture are then the most important functions of a State. It is evident that, in order to fulfil this function, the State must secure the spontaneous and free collaboration of all creative minds; and it is no less obvious that such a collaboration can only be secured under a system

The Principles

of freedom of thought, i.e. of free communication of thought and respect for the human conscience. It is sometimes suggested that freedom of thought is but freedom of error, and that culture is a matter of science and of accurate thinking which can easily proceed and thrive without freedom of thought. Experience shows that those for whom freedom of thought means freedom of error are precisely those who think so; and common sense points out that, since no one can be indisputably told off to define *ex cathedra* what is error and what is truth, what is culture and what is mere political discussion, the only satisfactory solution of the problem lies in freedom of thought. The relations between current political ideas and misconceptions on the one hand, and the deeper findings of selected minds on the other, are too numerous and subtle for any outsider to intervene with red pencil or scissors. Hence, in the practice of the dictatorial system, a severe index which drives into mental ostracism the most distinguished minds along with the boldest polemists of the nation; let alone the fact, more difficult to prove, yet equally evident to good observers, that mental activity pines in cages, however golden. Our conclusion will be, therefore, that freedom of thought is not less essential to the State than to the individual.

The requirements of the individual and of the State as to a considerable part of the problem of liberty are then in perfect harmony. This is a most important fact, for it is too readily assumed that the relationship which we have cautiously described as one of *polarity* is in reality one of pure and simple antagonism. That such antagonism exists up to a point between liberty and authority is evident, and we may have occasion to illustrate it later on; but the fact remains that, in many ways, the tendency to liberty in the individual is indispensable for the health of the State.

INEQUALITY AND CLASSES

This observation can be extended to some of the consequences of liberty which we have already discussed when dealing with this problem from the point of view of the individual. Thus inequality, which we saw as essential for a rich life and experience from the individual point of view, is, from the collective point of view, an invaluable asset to society. We do not mean by inequality the mere effects of natural differences on a scheme of life otherwise regulated by equalitarian principles. We mean precisely the complexity, the social landscape, the relief and the colour, the harmony and the disharmonies evolved by the interplay of natural differences, of the lag of tradition and the inertia of things, of the levelling efforts of rationalistic thought, of slow-rhythmed peasants and quick-living townsmen, the whole peppered over with the unaccountable, the unexpected, the exceptional, and the freak. That the pressure of economic conditions should have reduced this problem to one of classes, and the problem of classes to a mere matter of income, is natural but regrettable. Inequality is not to be measured along the vertical scale only and by the income unit only; it spreads sideways as much as up and down, in quality as much as in quantity, and the more dimensions it possesses the richer the life and the culture of the land and of the people which it graces with its presence.

It is difficult to see how the middle classes can be saved from destruction if they do not believe in themselves. They have submitted to constant abuse for nearly a century. They have reacted in the poorest possible way by creating middle-class unions and what-not. But the point is that practically the whole of Western civilization is due to them. Civilization means mostly the life of Western middle classes, and the arts, sciences, and amenities of the West are practically all the creations of middle-class men. Shakespeare, Cervantes, Goethe, Dante, Spinoza, Kant, Montesquieu, Galileo, Rembrandt, Voltaire, Velazquez, Volta, Pasteur, Hegel, Hernán Cortés, Napoleon, Gladstone, Bismarck, Descartes, Lincoln, Wilson, Einstein, names written down as they offer themselves to the imagination, were all middle-class men.

That there are aristocratic values in Western civilization—those, for instance, which have been evolved by luxury, the social creative power of which is considerable—no one doubts. That there are popular values in civilization such as those that are produced by craftsmanship, often due to popular inspiration, no one denies; but the fact remains that the centre of civilization, the store of it and the style of it are essentially bourgeois, and that it is to the bourgeoisie that we owe nearly all, if not all, the great human heights which have reflected the light of inspiration and genius. How can the middle classes be so dull as to allow in silence the vituperation and abuse of a class to which all that there is is due, all, including socialism?

The existence of classes is due to a number of causes, some of which have excited the legitimate wrath of generous hearts and the condemnation of enlightened minds. The problem is examined in its more fundamental aspects at a later stage in this work. It is here considered only in so far as it affects the question of the relationship between the individual and the State. Historical factors which in the European continent go back to feudalism and to conquest, while in ex-colonial and colonial territories they hail back to discovery, spoliation, or both, and in new countries to pioneering and to railway and land enterprises, have created a wholly unjustified and often unsocial land monopoly; cases of wholly criminal spoliation based on corruption of State institutions are far from unknown. The capitalistic system has led to a wage-war, while the objective complications of the relationship between wages, costs, and prices, combined with the effect of foreign competition, have in nearly every case worked on the side of the ruthless employer. There is therefore in the social fact of classes much that is illegitimate which the new State should endeavour to correct.

But classes do not result merely and solely from exploitation and from a kind of historical drag; they are being rapidly reformed in Soviet Russia through

The Principles

the action of natural forces which it is beyond the wit of man to correct. This is perhaps the moment to say that the literature about *oppressors* and *oppressed* is more respectable as evidence of good charitable feelings than of a sound penetrating intellect. There is no such thing as an oppressing *class*, since it is well known that the capitalists of industry are often recruited in the so-called *oppressed* class: we are simply in the presence of the effect of natural differences and of the tendency of nature to produce a small number of men gifted for economic enterprise. The fact has nothing to do with class, less now than ever; the dilution of ownership of the means of production amongst the masses, due to the growing importance of the system of shares and bonds for recruiting capital, shifts the stress of the problem from one of distribution of the profits drawn out of labour to one of industrial constitution and the government of industries. Add to this change in the aspect of the problem the further complications which arise from new factors brought to industry by insurance and taxation. Viewed in this light, in all its inextricable technical complication, the true, sober, and realistic way of looking at it, the problem becomes grotesquely out of relation with the class-struggle fallacy and is more apt to be solved, or at least mitigated in its evil effects through an all but scientific study entrusted to specialists used to handling cold mathematics than through the heated speeches to be heard in meetings, whether capitalistic or labour. Thus the class-struggle tactics and the classless State set up as the goal of socialism appear to us as closely interconnected errors to be explained perhaps as the consequences of the materialistic interpretation of history.

The fact that classes exist is but the social manifestation of a natural phenomenon, i.e. the existence of human beings endowed with a greater or lesser spirit of initiative on which, as on a more or less powerful stem, are engrafted combinations of qualities and defects—of *tendencies*, to use a neutral word—in unlimited numbers. Just as with a forehead, two eyes, a nose, two lips, a chin, and two cheeks, framed up with hair or with the lack thereof, nature can produce fifteen hundred millions of different faces, so by combining relatively small numbers of tendencies nature can produce fifteen hundred millions of different characters. To this variety, a variety of human situations must correspond. Does this mean that the working class must remain at the lower end of the social scale in order to collect the mentally and morally weaker individuals of the community? Not at all. Life is far more complex than that, and offers not a few middle-class positions more suitable for the mediocre, the sluggish, and the stupid than many a working-class situation. Moreover, unstable positions and "misfits" are an essential part of the scheme. Falls and rises must occur; they are the salt of life, the lessons of experience, and the process whereby society renews its personnel. In this wealth of life may be seen the fertile collaboration of the two antagonistic forces, ambition and necessity, the one drawing individuals upwards, the other driving them downwards, so

The Principles

long as they are allowed free play within the society. These forces can have free play only in a society in which there are a sufficient number of levels and in which the freedom of movement in the up-and-down direction has not been stifled by means of artificial measures. If necessity has been recognized from the point of view of the individual as indispensable for the fulfilment of man's destiny on earth, it will be found no less valuable from the point of view of the community as one of the constituent forces of society. Ambition, a natural tendency, drives men upwards in search of more responsibilities, i.e. of the higher liberties, which can only be attained at the cost of many of the lower ones. Necessity makes the slothful bear down and lose rank which indirectly secures the necessary staffing of the lower occupations, while the individual meets with his appropriate destiny.

We find thus that necessity is an essential spring in the machinery for adjusting functions to capacities and liberties to functions. Functional liberty is, as we have seen when dealing with it from the individual point of view, one of the planes of harmony between the claims of the individual and the claims of society. It is not disputed by any school of political thought—least of all by dictatorships, which essentially consist in the granting of an unlimited amount of strictly functional liberty to the dictator. But this observation is a quiet reminder that liberty, inequality, and the couple ambition-necessity are three powerful elements in the process whereby a society selects its leaders. We shall return to this problem. Here it may suffice to state that the vaster the three-dimensional field of inequality which a society evolves, the wider the range of human types amongst which it can select its leaders.

LIMITS TO LIBERTY

We must now bear in mind that, in the complex idea which we know as *authority*, we have detected an element inseparably connected with it in experience, though logically independent of it in theory, namely the tendency to individual liberty in the man who happens to wield political power at the time. Power is the sphere of action at the disposal of liberty. It is therefore only natural that men with a strong tendency to liberty should be ambitious, i.e. should seek to provide for themselves an ambit for positive power proportioned to their appetite for liberty, which usually is in its turn proportionate to the instinctive and intuitive perception of their own inner or natural powers. The difference between the arbitrary and, as the saying goes, "irresponsible" tyrant and the conscious statesman (whether a liberal democrat or a dictator) is that ambition in the latter seeks the higher liberties conscious of the sacrifice and the restraint of the lower liberties which creative power implies; while the former sees in power an unrestricted freedom for all his lower as well as his higher tendencies. This element, inherent, if not in authority, at any rate in the exercise of authority by a kind of natural contamination, is no doubt what gives to State authority its skeleton for resistance and its stamina for attack. We find again that omnipresent man in whom, when discussing finality, we saw the incarnation of everything there is in collective life.

It follows that in every manifestation of collective life, of whatever nature it be, whether nearer the individual or nearer the social pole, we are to expect that the tendency to liberty will work to the extreme limit of its possibilities, and that therefore, not merely when dealing with individuals as free agents without any social responsibilities, but also when considering them as social or political authorities, such as statesmen, employers, trade-union leaders, and foremen, the community must guard itself against the natural vigour of individual liberty acting in the first case as an excessively dispersive and in the second case as an excessively compressive force.

This raises the question: is the State entitled to react? Have we not agreed that things must be considered from the point of view of the individual, and that there must be as much liberty as possible? "As possible," we said. And the State, which, as we have seen, cannot thrive without individual liberty, is nevertheless entitled to set limits to it in order to guarantee first its own existence, then its proper mechanical working, finally, the fulfilment of its ends. At the outset it is evident that this discussion cannot lead us to any denial of essential liberty to the individuals, since we have already come to the conclusion that the State has no finality, and that therefore in the last resort the individual is not for the State but the State is for the individual.

Unanimous Organic Democracy

As for the first of the grounds on which the State is entitled to limit individual liberty, it goes without saying that no State can afford to allow any of its citizens to become so powerful that he may check its own authority. Needless to say, this elementary law of statecraft has been lamentably forgotten by liberal democracies, and there is no question that, on this ground, dictatorships would have a strong argument against democracies—if they could prove that they themselves were independent of the economic or military powers in their midst. This is in actual fact the most important of all political problems, for politics may be defined as the mechanics of social forces, and the most important problem in mechanics is to know where the strongest force is.

There is no general solution for this problem, which life presents under an infinite number of forms. But it may be safely asserted that no citizen should be allowed the liberty to accumulate financial and economic powers to an extent uncomfortable for the power of the State. This is a limitative principle, wholly empirical, which we must adapt to the circumstances of time and place in which it may have to be applied. It does not conflict with the existence of a wide margin of individual liberty nor with the exercise of private initiative within a wide range. It should suffice, however, to inspire legislation for curtailing the undue development of private fortunes, the unrestricted use of economic power over production, and the unchecked control over finance and credit—all of which, apart from their importance from this general political point of view, are, as we shall have occasion to see, measures to be taken also from the strictly economic point of view.

Though this principle of self-preservation should suffice in theory to guard against the evil effects of the accumulation of power by a few citizens, experience would probably suggest, and prudence advises, to associate it with adequate precautions against the use of individual power to secure control of important organs of collective life, such as municipal and national assemblies, public offices, and the Press. In this field the State has an evident right to control individual liberty.

So far the restrictive action of the State on individual liberty touches only on the closely political aspects of it. The State, however, on grounds of self-preservation can claim the right to curtail certain liberties which belong to the area of private behaviour. Since the State cannot be preserved apart from the community which it administers and represents, it must uphold the principles of ethics and the basic customs of its communities. Thus all legislation contains stipulations against actions which are either condemned by human ethics all over the world—such as murder—or against forms of life which, though not universally condemned, are rejected by the spirit of the time and place—such as polygamy in the twentieth-century West. This restriction of private liberty cannot be said to go against the essential rights of man to his experience, since it is only natural to expect that such an

Unanimous Organic Democracy

experience should form itself within the canvas of current ideas and customs.

But the most important claim of the State to limit individual liberty comes from its duty to ensure its proper mechanical working. The State is, in our view, not final but instrumental, yet this instrument exists for man. Its proper working is, therefore, of momentous importance. Given the intimate connection between the individual and the community, the individual would suffer deeply in body, mind, and spirit if the State collapsed and if the community lost thereby its means of expression and of consciousness. This matter, therefore, is crucial. It is on this spot that the roads fork apart; from here bigots of liberal democracy will have to travel along a lonely path. As for us, men of our century, we believe that, precisely because the State is for the individual in what concerns values, the individual must be for the State in what concerns functions. In one word, we are of opinion that the State cannot tolerate that its own workings should be thrown out of gear by high or low.

All that is mechanical in life must proceed without interruption. The State is in great part machinery. The community is in great part machinery also. In so far as we are pieces of that machinery our business is to perform the duties assigned to us. While the precise form under which this principle is to be applied will have to be examined in each particular case, the principle itself is quite clear: no society can work without order, hierarchy, continuity, and discipline. The State must see to it that these

The Principles

conditions prevail, and no theory of individual liberty may be valid against such a duty because no essential individual liberty is involved.

If the nineteenth century has allowed its machinery to be transformed into an arsenal out of which capital and labour make projectiles for civil strife, it is due to the fact that liberal democracies did not sincerely envisage private interest as a mere stimulus for automatically ensuring public interest, but felt in their hearts that it was but a nice fig-leaf for private greed. The nineteenth-century State lacked moral authority to put a stop to the unseemly behaviour of its citizens battling over its body for the distribution of its life-blood. The economic State —nay, more generally still, the functional State— must be authoritarian. It can tolerate neither strikes nor lock-outs, neither militant associations of workmen nor militant associations of employers. Still less, of course, can it countenance that its own workmen, postmen, schoolmasters should form associations based on their function and with the object of controlling it. The so-called conquests of liberty have nothing at all to do with that liberty which is an essential condition for the life of man. They are born of a hopeless misconception of what liberty is and of what the State is. They are not democratic but demagogic. They must go.

There is no closer, no more intimate relation between economics and politics than that which sets in between the material basis of a man's life and his higher liberty, or rather the exercise thereof. The State, in its respect for individual liberty, is bound to allow as much free play as possible to private initiative in the economic as in any other form of life. The State also, as any unbiased mind must recognize, has much to gain from the play of private initiative within its body politic. Nevertheless, the State is bound to limit private initiative not merely in order to avoid the accumulation by a few citizens of so much power that the collective machinery may be thrown out of gear, but also in order to ensure the smooth working of this machinery against caprice, combines, the political use of industrial functions and power, or the miscarriage of its general power of economic direction; finally, the State cannot stand by while the working of the law of necessity drags down to utter misery, destitution, and possibly crime the less gifted and fortunate of its citizens. The adjustment of all these different claims is one of the problems of the modern State. Whatever the solution to be found for it, a solution which is bound to differ in practice from one country to another, it is clear that the State will have to retain private initiative and to harness it to public use more closely than is done nowadays.

It is obvious that the State cannot countenance actions contrary to its spirit, still less organizations which aim at performing such actions. Thus, for instance, liberty of thought does mean that all ideas may be freely discussed, even the most absurd; common sense will deal with them; but if liberty of thought would let pass a cool discussion on murder, the State cannot tolerate either murder or the publication of writings advocating it. Similarly, the

State, in the name of freedom of thought, will tolerate writings against freedom of thought, but cannot tolerate that doctrines against freedom of thought should be taught in its schools; for teaching is action and not thought, and the State cannot tolerate action against its fundamental principles. Or again, the State may look on while a party is formed for altering its fundamental principles, aiming at establishing, for instance, a dictatorship, whether of the hammer and scythe, or of the sword, the swastika or the fascio; but the moment such a party organizes its adherents into a more or less regular legion or troop, and preaches violence as a method of political change, the State is entitled—indeed, bound—to intervene and to outlaw the party.

It is useless to argue against this doctrine on grounds of tolerance. Universal and unreserved tolerance is an abstraction and has never had any practical existence. Intolerance is but the shadow cast by the light of faith. Where there is faith there is intolerance. We moderns, when we pride ourselves on our tolerance, whether we know it or not, are priding ourselves on our lack of faith. Yet we are neither faithless nor tolerant. What happens is that our faith has shifted, and our intolerance with it. Nowadays we believe in two gods only—our nation and its bank. An offence against our country, or a threat against our bank credit—will either of these find us tolerant? A community is always intolerant towards doctrines or actions which threaten its fundamental beliefs. The modern State will be intolerant towards those who prevent its proper working and towards those who threaten its essential constitution.

STATISTIC DEMOCRACY AND ORGANIC DEMOCRACY

All that precedes goes to show that the State must be conceived as the manifestation of an organic, and not merely a statistical or numerical, democracy. The assumption that government by the people means government by the sum total of the inhabitants of the nation or by a majority of them—an assumption which, however absurd, is at the basis of the actual working and even of the current thinking of our liberal democracies, is sufficient to explain the plight in which they find themselves. Collective life is still conceived of as a kind of prolongation of the life of the bush. Instead of seeing and understanding it from the point of view of a higher unity, as might be expected from beings endowed with reason, we allow it to drift as a purely mechanical phenomenon in the direction of the force which will "result" from the "composition" of all the individual and group forces present. In recent times such an attitude has even been raised to the rank of political theory by those who deny the State any specific function or dignity above and apart from other groups in the State. We do not propose to discuss the theoretical aspects of this question, although we do not take the view that it is useless to set up a theory as to what relations of power should be, irrespective of what these relations of power are, for this view would

The Principles

imply that human thought has no influence over human evolution. Modest as we may be about the influence of books over people and of people—particularly those who read books—over events, we would not write books at all if we did not think that it is in the mind that the origin of all political forces resides. We have defined politics as the mechanics of political life, but the forces of political life are all moral forces and they rest on conviction. It is therefore fundamental that our ideas on the State should be sound, for, if they are, the chances of the State itself being sound are greatly enhanced.

Now it seems evident to us that liberal democracies have altogether disregarded the organic aspect of society, first by granting the principle of separation between economics and politics while empirically bowing to their inevitable co-operation, very much as a lady who having refused marriage accepts a liaison; and then by evolving principles and practices of political life too crudely based on mere numbers.

Liberal-democratic leaders should bear in mind that dictators have always benefited by this confusion between *people* and *organized nation*, which they have of course made systematic, outdoing whatever there may be of demagogic in democratic practices. Thus the plebiscite, which we find at the origin of all dictatorships as a kind of popular baptism, is but a *reductio ad absurdum* of universal suffrage. The three steps which took Napoleon from the Republic to the Empire (Constitution of the year VIII, change from the temporary Consulate to the life Consulate year X, and the transformation of the life Consulate

Unanimous Organic Democracy

into the Empire in the year XII) were submitted to the direct popular vote; the basis of the Soviet dictatorship is also a kind of plebiscite, i.e. the election to the Panrussian Congress; and of recent years the German dictatorship has conquered power and confirmed itself in it by plebiscite mass votes. The direct method of popular consultation of the electorate is therefore a caricature of democracy, not real democracy. It rests on mass, not on an organic nation.

When we pass from political theory to the actual facts, the first thing we observe is that the majority of human beings are not interested enough in politics to trouble about them. There is a gradation of interest which goes from leadership, through active participation in political action, attending meetings, talking over a glass of beer, reading newspapers, not worrying at all, to finally complete ignorance of the very existence of politics. In most countries, even the most enlightened from the political point of view, it will be found that by far the greater majority of people are to be met in the lower grades of the scale from "the talking over a glass of beer" downwards. Liberal democracies, through the personal competition of candidates and the political competition of parties, worry this majority out of the peaceable enjoyment of its a-political life. This is a dubious blessing both for the liberal-democratic system and for the nations which apply it. Citizenship is a vocation, and good active citizenship cannot be expected of the human beings—some of them delightful—who do not feel so inclined. Political institutions should take this fact into consideration. Thus, for instance, any efforts at converting the indifferent to active citizenship should not be so strenuous as to force the inclination of the sluggish. There is no drawback whatsoever in the fact that the nation carries a dead weight of politically passive people who, in other walks of life than the merely political one, are by no means a dead weight, but, on the contrary, may be very much alive. At any rate, it is a lesser danger than the forcing of them into political life against the grain.

The true interest of a democracy may perhaps lie, not in forcing people to the polls, but, on the contrary, in carefully regulating entry to citizenship. There is no real reason why active citizenship should be considered *a priori* as the right of an inhabitant of a country. The establishing of tests of capacity is a matter which deserves careful attention. There is no doubt that some such tests have been used by hypocritical democracies as an anti-democratical weapon. But the abuse of an institution is not a sufficient argument against its utility.

This restriction of citizenship so as to gain in quality what is lost in quantity would contribute in great part to correct the drawbacks of current democracies. The incompetence of the citizen and voter would diminish in two ways: by detaching from the electorate a mass of indifferent people whose very passivity argues incompetence; and by raising the level of the active citizens and their information through the very means that would be used in selecting them. The man who is easily corrupted, the man of short views, the egoist, the trifler would disappear or become more rare in public life. The first step, therefore, in the creation of an organic democracy might well be to restrict citizenship, conceding it as a dignity only to those who showed themselves both desirous and worthy of it.

This would be an excellent foundation on which to establish the selective machinery of the government. For it is evident, although it has been lamentably forgotten by liberal democracies, *that a government is always an oligarchy and ought to be always an aristocracy*. A provocative statement perhaps, but one which can be justified. That a government is an oligarchy flows as an inevitable consequence from the nature of things, since the word *oligarchy* means government *by the few*, and it is a sheer absurdity that government should be exercised by the many. What distinguishes the different forms of government is not that, in an autocracy, fewer persons govern than in a democracy; that may be the case, but it is not essential; the real difference lies in the method of selecting the few who, in either case, govern. In an autocracy, the selection is made by the autocrat, or more often by a small group which exercises authority in his name, whilst in a democracy the people intervene more or less in the selection. But the true problem underlying that of the form of government is: how to ensure that the government *is* an aristocracy. And do not let the democratic reader be put off by this word which has been so much calumniated and corrupted by a century of misinterpretation. *Aristocracy* means, after all, that the power is in the hands of the best. And who would be bold enough to set himself up against such a doctrine?

In the present world the only peoples who are, or at any rate try or profess to be, governed by an aristocracy are the several peoples federated under the Union of Socialist Sovietist Republics. Power in the Soviet Union is the privilege and the exclusive responsibility of the Communist Party, which is understood as an aristocracy in that

(*a*) It is very carefully recruited;
(*b*) It is severely inspected and periodically cleansed;
(*c*) Its members are expected to study public affairs and give time to them;
(*d*) The salary of any official belonging to the party cannot exceed a very small minimum, whatever the rank or responsibility expected of him.

We do not advocate this system for Western countries, but we do believe that the principle that public affairs should be the privilege of an aristocracy, in the original sense of the word, must be adopted by all democracies if they are to survive. This is a further reason why a selective system, beginning at the very basis of citizenship, would appear to be indispensable. So far, party strife has been directed towards criticism of party doctrines or of party leaders; the absence of any outward code of public conduct for the mere citizen has made it impossible to bring out into the light many of the worst features of democracy which should be traced to the people itself and to its unsatisfactory conception of the theory and practice of citizenship. A minimum standard of citizenship must be set up if we aim at raising the level of public ethics and efficiency in our democracies.

The selective process thus made much easier by a selection at the base should, of course, proceed at every degree of the hierarchy. The methods at present applied for the choice of the representatives of the people should be thoroughly overhauled. Two schools of thought are in the field: the first advocates the current method on the basis of territory; the second advocates the functional method on the basis of profession. This second school aims at correcting the obvious defect of democracies, namely, that they usually select their political staff, both representative and executive, without due regard for competence and assuming that any man is competent for anything. The issue "democracy versus efficiency" has been alive for many a year, and becomes daily more pressing as technique invades wider and wider areas of the political ground. But its best solution may lie in a middle course, which would be based on the fundamental division of public activities between function and value. In a previous chapter we have come to the conclusion that the citizen is for the State but the State is for man, or, in other words, *that in all that concerns functions the individual must serve the State, while in all that concerns values the State must*

The Principles

serve the individual. From this distinction a line may be drawn between the activities of the State which belong to the material world and the activities of the State which belong to the moral world. In each of these two spheres a different kind of organization should be adopted. In the material State a professional criterion for the selection of leaders would be but natural; in the moral State selection should follow the territorial line. In both cases selection would have to be based on two clear and simple ideas: the electorate should know the area of problems on which the chosen leader is to act or to deliberate; the electorate should also know the candidates from the public point of view, and not from the point of view of the more or less selfish advantages which they would be in a position to offer if elected.

It is obvious that a democracy judges itself by the leaders it selects. There is no golden rule for finding the best. The wisest systems imaginable would fail in the hands of a stupid, a corrupt, or a sluggish people; but the simple general ideas here put forward should help to a better selection than at present obtains in most countries. Even so, nothing can be expected without the collaboration of time. It may even happen that a happy combination of historical facts converging from many quarters of collective life, some possibly quite undemocratic, may produce an excellent government which will ensure the success of a democracy. Thus, the England of the late nineteenth century, an admirably governed country, owed its luck to the existence of an idle class of landed gentry which happened to be public-spirited—a clear case in which inequality led to a good choice of leadership and undemocratic conditions secured a prosperous and successful democracy.

LIBERTY AND ECONOMY

Of all the activities of Nature, that which sets limits to the intellect of man with the firmest, if the most elusive, hand is perhaps the economic order of things. The infinite of astronomic spaces and the anti-infinite of atomic arcana have lent themselves more easily to the penetration of men's minds than these everyday creations of man which we call production, distribution, and consumption. It is, therefore, but natural that this sphere should have seen the most heroic attempts at scientific generalization and the most dramatic failures therein. Two such heroic attempts dominate the others: one which boldly asserts that, if the natural tendencies of economic life are allowed free play, since the equilibrium of economic life is stable, any slight disturbance which deviates from it sets at work forces which tend to restore it: therefore, *let be*. The other asserts no less boldly and scientifically that, as a fatal result of capitalistic industrialization, a class-war will set in which will bring about a brief period of socialism, after which the classless State will flourish for ever among for ever happy men.

One thing is certain: that neither of these two

theories is *science*. The world of men is governed by many natural laws, amongst which the natural laws of economics, whatever they are, are a relatively important but not a predominant group. So that any attempt to solve the problem of collective life on economic principles is, in itself, a mistake; over and above which the further mistake is made of trying to solve economic life on one single economic principle. We take the opposite view on both questions: we believe that economic matters must be organized on wider principles than mere economics; and we believe that no single economic principle is complex enough to fit life, ever original and spontaneous.

The most important question to ask when dealing with the economic organization of society is: What about individual liberty? The preceding pages have been devoted to an analysis of the essential aspects of liberty. These aspects are, of course, of a spiritual character. Now, the links between individual liberty and the economic conditions in which life is lived are most intimate. The Marxist school is right in its critical, if not in its constructive, aspects. Economic slavery and individual liberty do not go together. We should not, however, exaggerate this argument. The *economic weight* of man, i.e. the fact that he must satisfy a scale of wants by no means uniform for all men, before he can think of freedom, is one of the permanent forces of life. To imagine that the employer is free from economic weight is to think that a ball bouncing has no material weight. In fact, since the employer has more wants to satisfy on the consumption side of his account and a far greater need of capital on the productive side than any of his men, it would appear that men may lose in liberty as they rise in apparent ease. This is a fact which many a bourgeois must have experienced. Liberty, therefore, is a tendency which has to insert itself into a complicated set of forces acting in convergent or divergent directions in relation to it, the most important of which is precisely that which we have described as economic weight. The yearning for unfettered liberty which lives in every man's breast is but the spiritual counterpart of the yearning to fly, free from the fetters of gravity, which is also one of man's dreams. That the progress of technique which has conquered material weight may some day conquer economic weight is a pious wish, but no more. Thus, we must accept this natural limitation of our liberty. But, as we have already seen, both in the higher and final interests of man and in the lower and instrumental interest of the State, we must seek to reduce it to a minimum. Two ways lead to that end: the first through the individual, the second through the community. The individual can reduce his economic weight just as a lady reduces her "line," by diminishing his material requirements. Diogenes in his barrel is here the model. We thus come by another way to the conclusion at which we had just arrived, namely, that liberty does not necessarily grow with wealth, or, in other words, that liberty is not in the least a simple fact of life but the result of an equilibrium so complex and unpredictable that it can only be estimated by the

The Principles

person directly concerned. At the collective end individual liberty can be altered, by means of economic fetters, within a fairly wide range according to the political and economic system which is the setting of the citizen's life.

It is here perhaps that the crux of the matter lies, for it is here that Marxism joins issue with capitalism. The trend of history, however, has led the world away from pure capitalism. The theory of *laissez faire* may be as perfect as its advocates assert, but it is gone for ever. What actually remains in all countries but Russia is a hotch-potch, the result of the fermentation of economic liberalism, by the action of socialistic, technical, and nationalistic ferments. Marxism, which in this matter represents order and rationalism as opposed to anarchy and intuition, would have conquered the field long ago if there had been no more powerful holders of the position than capitalists and their intellectual servants. It is true that, ultimately, the position is held by the military forces of the capitalistic-socialistic nations. But these military forces would have gone over to the other side if the doctrines of socialism had really conquered people's minds. They have conquered many minds, and the psychological study of this conquest would be fascinating; but the bulk of opinion in the West remains unconvinced by Marxism, nor is the experience of Russia likely to convince them.

The root of this opposition to Marxism in the main body of Western opinion evidently lies in this: that private enterprise is one of the primary necessities of man, or, in other words, essential to our purpose, that private enterprise in economic affairs is one of the inherent forms of liberty considered as the ambit of that individual experience in which we have seen the main aim of man and, therefore, of the State to consist. The importance both theoretical and practical of this fact cannot be exaggerated. For, on theoretical grounds, it condemns Marxism as contrary to the right relationship between the individual and the State, and therefore as a form of State which the State has no right to adopt; while on practical grounds it permits the forecast that Marxist experiments are doomed to be wrecked on the rock of human psychology which will revolt against them.

It follows that whatever considerations we may have to add from other points of view to our scheme of collective life, the economy of our modern State must rest on private initiative. But, as we are working with living materials, it is safe to assume that every affirmation must bring forth its own negation, for all in life is ebb and flow, and of course, once private initiative has been well established as the axis of our economic State, we must proceed to treat it as engineers treat an axis, i.e. to hold it at its two extremes so that it remains true to itself, to hold it though not so fast that it cannot revolve, yet fast enough to prevent it from getting out of gear. For private initiative, unlimited, is in effect the most dangerous enemy of the State. We have more than once met with this thought that the State cannot afford to allow any citizen to become too powerful.

The Principles

We know also that the State cannot afford to allow a completely free play to "negative private initiative," i.e. such unrestricted and uncontrolled necessity as would let fall into the hell of destitution, vice and crime, the victims of their own sloth, or possibly of unfavourable circumstances. Though this scheme of the State may not appeal to theoretical minds, who require a regularly constructed chessboard of principles, such an empirically adjusted application of the simple rule of private initiative seems to us more adapted to the theoretical requirements of individual finality as well as to the practical requirements of human psychology than any cut-and-dried social and economic system.[1]

Any measures calculated to limit the excesses of private initiative will indirectly correct the excesses of social inequality. What is the main objection levelled against inequality? Not that it allows the rights of the capable, but that it grants the incapable an undue amount of social influence if they happen to be born in the upper spheres of society. The English, in this as in most collective matters such consummate masters that their wisdom is far above that of the other nations and therefore remains inaccessible and useless to them, understand that the scions of the upper families, even though moderately able (English for hopelessly stupid), have some contribution to make to the community

---

[1] It will be observed that private initiative satisfies the two conditions of individual liberty: that it be granted to him who feels the need of it, and that it be not inflicted on him who has felt "the weight of too much liberty." It is an automatic criterion.

in that they give mass, inertia, and, so to speak, fat to the body politic in those parts which are the storehouse of tradition. I recall that once in Oxford I happened to be discussing educational matters with the head of a college known, of course, for its scholarship, but still more so for the blue blood of its students. And as I suggested that, in view of the queue of applicants, the college could well afford to raise the level of its entrance examination, I was suavely and rightly rebuked with the remark that, since the sons of dukes and earls would, in any case, belong to the governing class, it was just as well that they should spend a few years in college and get at any rate subconsciously educated. It would be too much to expect that such masterpieces of political wisdom should be appreciated beyond the Channel by any but a few specialists of English life. It is, therefore, prudent to provide for a system whereby the upper ranks of the community are renewed so soon as their occupants are no longer able to stand on their own legs at such heights.

But the limitations of private initiative do not merely apply to the power which any one citizen may come to accumulate through the handling of economic and financial sources of production. The actual ownership of these sources of production is perhaps less important than socialist authorities incline to think. If the enterprises are very big they are owned in most cases by a considerable number of shareholders and bondholders; if they are small they may be in the hands of one man. But, in either case, the important point is not the legal ownership but the power of control over the industry which ownership may or may not imply. Now, this power, through the growing complexity of economic relations, is rapidly diminishing; much of it has passed to the banks, much to the industrial associations of manufacturers of which often the individual manufacturer is but a kind of local agent, and, finally, a good share of it has gone over to the trades unions. All this process takes place somewhat blindly, because there is no central agency to direct it in its happy-go-lucky evolution.

The modern State cannot let its economic and financial evolution go adrift. Economics and finance are not a matter of opinion; they are a matter of careful husbandry based on information and expert knowledge. Thus, the amount of money available, its rate, the balance of production, both within its several branches and with consumption, the handling of the deviations from natural economy which capital and its influence over politics may have produced, the question whether workers have anything to gain by forcing salaries up instead of seeking other benefits such as insurance, the bearing of unemployment on salaries, the relations between trade and industry, all these matters which are nowadays bones for political dogs to fight over in the public square, should be put back where they belong, to the quiet and impartial study of disinterested minds. This is the real liberty, and not the so-called liberty invoked in order to paralyse the nation's life by civil struggles and wars. It is necessary, therefore, to co-ordinate private initiative in a general scheme of national economy which may, in some future but not too future date, be co-ordinated in its turn with a larger scheme of world economy.

SOVEREIGNTY

We have all along assumed that the State is entitled to take final decisions binding on all citizens. Though this assumption has been challenged by certain modern schools of thought, it is difficult to see how collective life can be conceived without some authority expressing the unity of the national group. Either we admit the existence of the nation or we do not. If we do not, the matter must be shifted to whichever group—small or big—represents the community. But if we think (*a*) that, as indeed is obvious, the nation is there and not in the least ready to be removed from the surface of the earth, and (*b*) that it is the most convenient setting for individual activities, then we must grant to the nation its corresponding institution, the State.

We assert, then, that the State must have sovereignty, i.e. that in matters of collective life it must have the last word. We do not see in the State a kind of mystical entity, a *deus ex machina* that ordinary mortals must obey out of a philosophical faith; nor do we think it is just a group amongst others that must be obeyed because it happens to be stronger, when it is stronger. In our opinion the sovereignty of the State is a pure matter of common sense. Men, whatever their differences on points of detail, must agree on a minimum of rules to carry on collective life. Let us for instance, but only for instance, suppose that the rule is adopted that the opinion of the majority is to prevail; State sovereignty in this case would mean that it is incumbent on the State to see that the rule is applied, since it has been adopted. Discussions on the sovereignty of the State are apt to be unduly loaded with theory. Any sailor knows there must be a captain, any footballer too. The State is the captain of the team. Of course there are weak States in which the army officers, the bishops, the trade unions, the bankers, the opera ballet dancers are more powerful than the executive. But in what way does that conflict with the commonsense view that the State *must* have authority? The assertion that a captain must have authority implies that there are captains who do not possess that gift or circumstances in which they lose it. Sovereignty thus means the attribute of the entity which has the last word, and in every civilized nation that attribute corresponds to the State.

It is the sad privilege of our age to have witnessed a return of political opinion to the era at which State sovereignty and force were thought to be one. Force as the basis of the State is a pragmatic truth. In the end it comes to that. But the distinction between the *is* and the *should be* is one of the attributes of man that men can only give up to their dishonour. And the *should be* is one of the forces which shape the *is*. While it is true that the State which actually lives is that which, for good or for evil, has force on its side, it is also true that that force which looks so physical is in reality a moral force. It depends on the convictions of the men that compose it. Therefore, the opinions which are taught in schools, in the Press, through the radio, and the cinema, and, last but not least, through the direct perception of national realities by men, will sooner or later colour the conviction of the armed forces and determine the regime of the State. Hence the importance of a sound doctrine of the State, but also the still greater importance of the behaviour, competence, and devotion of the leaders. No people will go to the trouble and danger of a revolution if it is well governed. Thus we come by another route to our previous conclusion, that a government must be an aristocracy. For the consent of the governed, which is, in the last resort, the basis of the moral force behind physical force, will be granted by men only when the superiority of those who govern is well established.

But here some caution may be necessary, for this word *sovereignty*, borrowed from the vocabulary of absolute monarchy, is a stranger in that of democracy and is apt to be misunderstood. It has a most unfortunate ring of absolutism. It may, therefore, be worth while to attempt a close delineation of its frontiers. In our opinion the sovereignty of the modern State differs according to whether we consider internal affairs of an economic character; internal affairs of a political and moral character; and external affairs.

As for internal affairs of an economic nature, in

The Principles

our modern world complete economic liberty is a material impossibility. Even so, as we have shown, it is as important to the State as to the individual that the community should be so organized as to allow the maximum measure of liberty compatible with our times. But the State must be empowered to direct the financial and economic life of the country and to adjust it to that of the world in general. This is inevitable. Whatever the details of the economic organization of the nation it is obvious that leadership can belong to the State alone. Indeed, in this connection, the most urgent duty of the modern State is to rescue its lost sovereignty in matters of money and credit from the grip of the private banks which have been gradually and quietly absorbing it. No citizen, nor group of citizens, can justify action against the State in economic matters. The nation is something other than a going concern, and that is why the functional State, the nothing-but-functional State, does not satisfy us; but in so far as the nation is a going concern the economic life of the community must be regulated on grounds of efficiency, and therefore on the basis of expert authority, competence, and hierarchy.

The sovereignty of the State in matters of a moral and political order cannot be so complete. On this plane the State is the servant of the individual. This is, as we have seen, the plane of individual liberty, that in which the individual seeks his experience. The sovereignty of the State does not cease to be necessary; but, while on the economic plane it directs, and if necessary executes, its decisions, here it acts solely in order to secure its own proper existence against the disruptive effects of individual liberty, abstaining from all intervention in the higher and more private forms of that liberty.

The idea of State sovereignty takes on its most objectionable form when applied to foreign affairs, for in this field the State has come gradually to establish a position of wholly unmoral behaviour which tells heavily both against the individual and against world peace. It is easy to see how this situation came about as a consequence of the disruption of the Holy Roman Empire and of the rise of the great European nations in the fifteenth and sixteenth centuries.

With the birth of a new international spirit having for the first time a world-wide basis, territorially, racially, and spiritually, the limitations of State sovereignty in external affairs stand out clearly. When discussing the problem of finality, we saw that the State must serve the individual and is, hierarchically, below the individual in all that pertains to values. Now there is no more important value in man than that of manhood, since it comprises them all. Without man no Truth, no Goodness, no Beauty. Therefore manhood is the value of values, the fountain of values, the hope of values, and before manhood the State must bow.

But manhood is common to all men and recognizes no frontiers. Just as the State is the community polarized to the citizen, the background of organized collective life against which the citizen can be understood, so mankind, organized mankind, is the community polarized to man, the background of organized collective life on which man can be understood. The State must therefore insert itself hierarchically in organized mankind; it occupies, indeed, a high rank in this organization. It is the setting of a local culture adapted to a human culture and transmits the more remote values thereof to its own citizens. It is the centre of a local organization linked up with a world organization that is to be, of which the League of Nations is the first timid but hopeful attempt.

It follows that individual liberty must remain intact in all that pertains to the relations between the world-citizen and the world-State. It is foolish to speak of a super-State, but it is foolish not to see that a world-State has become necessary, indeed that it already exists. It exists so soon as the consciousness of belonging to organized mankind is established in a sufficient number of human beings to constitute a nucleus of world-consciousness. In these conditions the national State cannot overstep the limits fixed for it by the higher relation which unites man to man, higher though, may be, looser than that which unites citizen to citizen, just as the relation of man to mankind is higher, though perhaps less intense, than patriotism.

In actual practice the new position amounts to the appearance of a number of new rights and duties:

Unanimous Organic Democracy

(1) The State has to limit its sovereignty in foreign affairs within the framework of international law and ethics. A first code of international law is in being in the Covenant of the League of Nations.

(2) The State must limit its sovereignty as regards the individual in that it should no longer demand military service for any war, but only for wars within the principles of international law and ethics.

(3) The individual should have the right to refuse to serve the State in wars waged in violation of the principles of international law and ethics.

This third rule raises the question of conscientious objection, one of the most difficult of adjustment between individual liberty and State sovereignty. The attitude of the absolute conscientious objector, the man who will fight under no conditions whatever, seems to me mistaken. Not only does it reveal an intellectual stubbornness and pride very much at variance with the religious principle which such objectors usually profess, but it amounts to taking the smooth and rejecting the rough of collective association. The logical absolute conscientious objector should have to make a strict vow of poverty and live on the begging-bowl. But the inhabitant of a metropolis, brimful of the wealth acquired by economic and military power, taking his fair—at times perhaps his unfair—share of the spoils, while looking away with horror from the means wherewith they have been acquired, and are

The Principles

kept, cannot be considered as a consistent champion of noble principles.

There are two more arguments against the absolute conscientious objector. The first is that justice and the order which is established on it must at times be maintained by force. Aggression must be repelled. The breaker of the peace must be punished. The ultra-pacifist who enjoys the benefits of that order must collaborate in vindicating it if and when called upon to do so. Finally, the admission in law of the scruple of conscience against all fighting would inevitably create a premium on cowardice. Conscientious objectors, as seen in England during the last war, are men for the greater part wrong-headed but right-hearted, of great courage, both physical and moral, and capable of enduring the sufferings and humiliations which their attitude brings on them. But behind them the cowardly citizens would flock under pretexts of simulated, imagined, and even *sublimated* scruples. The admission of absolute conscientious objection in law is therefore both a theoretical and a practical impossibility.

But this does not mean that, in concrete circumstances and on certain well-defined grounds, conscientious objection cannot be admitted. The matter was put clearly enough, though in the language of his time, by the true founder of the law and ethics of international life, Father Vitoria, in his lectures to the students of Salamanca. This admirable master laid down two principles which, when translated from the language of dogmatic religion into terms of modern law, are irrefutable:

Many doubts are suggested by what has just been said. In the first place, there is a doubtful point in connection with the justice of a war, whether it be enough for a just war that the prince believes himself to have a just cause. On this point let my first proposition be: This belief is not always enough. And for proof I rely, first, on the fact that in some matters of less moment it is not enough either for a prince or for private persons to believe that they are acting justly. This is notorious, for their error may be vincible and deliberate, and the opinion of the individual is not enough to render an act good, but it must come up to the standard of a wise man's judgment, as appears from *Ethics*, book 2. Also the result would otherwise be that very many wars would be just on both sides, for although it is not a common occurrence for princes to wage war in bad faith, they nearly always think theirs is a just cause. In this way all belligerents would be innocent and it would not be lawful to kill them. Also, were it otherwise, even Turks and Saracens might wage just wars against Christians, for they think they are thus rendering God service.

Second doubt: Whether subjects are bound to examine the cause of a war or whether they may serve in the war without any careful scrutiny thereof, just as the lictors had to enforce the praetor's decree without questioning. On this doubt let my first proposition be: If a subject is convinced of the injustice of a war, he ought not to serve in it, even on the command of his prince. This is clear, for no one can authorize the killing of an innocent person. But in the case before us the enemy are innocent. Therefore they may not be killed. Again, a prince sins when he commences a war in such a case. But "not only are they who commit

The Principles

such things worthy of death, but they, too, who consent to the doing thereof" (*Romans*, ch. 1). Therefore soldiers also are not excused when they fight in bad faith. Again, it is not lawful to kill innocent citizens at the prince's command. Therefore not aliens either.

Hence flows the corollary that subjects whose conscience is against the justice of a war may not engage in it, whether they be right or wrong. This is clear, for "whatever is not of faith is sin" (*Romans*, ch. 14).[1]

These principles provide a clear and convenient solution of the most vexed question of conscientious objection. The objection of conscience based on the second principle of Father Vitoria is essentially right. No State has the right to force its citizens to violate their conscience to that extent. The difficulty raised by the question: "What is a just war?" and even more so that raised by the question: "Who is to define a war as just?" have been removed by the existence of the League of Nations. Citizens might therefore be admitted to register *beforehand* and in time of peace their intention not to serve in wars which have been declared "unjust" by the Council of the League or by the Hague Court. The matter may seem at first sight purely platonic or academic. It is not. For, to begin with, it is in the best interests of peace or, what is ultimately the same, of world co-operation, that as many positions and habits of thought as possible should be taken on the basis of the world State. It is only by creating a kind of tissue of thoughts, actions, and emotions of a world

[1] Vitoria: *De Jure Belli*. Edited by Ernest Nys in the series, *The Classics of International Law*, page 173, paragraphs 20, 22, and 23.

character that we may hope to evolve that international Community without which it is useless to expect peace among peoples. The existence of a universal register of world citizens who would have undertaken not to fight in an unjust war but, on the other hand, to fight in a just war, would constitute a powerful deterrent against international aggression. Further, it is evident that the recognition in law of conscientious objection thus limited and defined must involve as an inevitable consequence the establishing of international protection for the citizen against his own national State in the case of possible violation of this human privilege.

THE TOTALITARIAN STATE AND THE UNANIMOUS ORGANIC DEMOCRACY

The methods which the dictators of our age have applied to set up the totalitarian State prevent many open minds from realizing the positive element contained in the idea itself. The nations of Europe, whether we take the England of the time of the great Elizabeth, the Spain of Charles V and Philip II, or the France of Louis XIV, only reached their plenitude in the form of totalitarian States. We moderns have been living under the tyranny of Darwin, who in his turn put into modern language a doctrine as old as Aristotle. Our subconscious attitude in political questions has been modelled on this conception and conceived of progress (whatever be the meaning we give to this word) as the son of strife. We all believed that, for a community to live and progress, it was indispensable that there should be within it at least two antagonistic political opinions.

But with the advent of socialism the idea began to circulate that parties and their modes of thought were but the political *forms* of economic *realities*: thus the conservative party would correspond to capitalism and ownership of the soil; the liberal to the liberal professions and to the middle classes; and the socialist party to the manual worker. And this idea, which has been gradually penetrating contemporary political thought far beyond the boundaries of the socialism within which it was born, is producing disastrous effects, so disastrous indeed that our civilization is threatened with destruction unless, to save it, we are prepared to sacrifice the Darwinian political system and turn towards a modern conception related to the totalitarian State: that of the unanimous organic democracy.

For this is the situation: the workers no longer feel that the conservative and liberal parties—condemned together as bourgeois parties—sincerely believe what they say or even what they think; on the contrary, the workers hold that the bourgeois parties are using their ideas as smoke-screens of political thought in order to defend their social and economic privileges. Our civilization is, then, menaced by a schism within it, a divorce of heart and mind between its working and its bourgeois classes.

There cannot be a fact of greater gravity, for

Unanimous Organic Democracy

civilization is a matter of unanimity and in it must participate consciously and voluntarily all those whom it includes. If, as the masses awake, they are not absorbed *pari passu* into the system of principles and beliefs which constitutes our civilization, it is evident that our civilization is doomed to perish, since sooner or later the masses will rebel against an order which they neither understand nor accept and which they do not respect; and, as the numbers are on their side, they must perforce win.

"And what of it?" might ask an impartial and objective observer, standing neutral between the different classes of society. But he would be mistaken. For we know already that the masses are, of themselves, by their very nature, incapable of constituting a State. Their victory would mean, therefore, either a victory for chaos, destructive of civilization, or a passing phase of disorder giving way to a new body of leaders.

But then, if the transformation of our present society, assumed incapable of absorbing the masses, into another capable of absorbing them could be done under the direction of our present leaders, the world would be saved the revolutionary phase, as well as that of creating new leaders and that of trial, doubt and possible failure of these new leaders in their effort to create a new society.

From all of which it follows that it is the imperative duty of the directing classes of our actual civilization to absorb the masses as they awaken to public life.

But absorb them into what? Certainly not into the capitalistic State; for the order created by capitalism no longer satisfies the intelligent man and is as little satisfactory to the worker. In order that the State may be able to absorb the masses into a community, it must first be the sincere representative of that community and must see itself from the point of view of the common interest. The State, therefore, must be a true Republic.

Now, in a true Republic fully constituted as such, there would be very little space to spare for political parties; for most of the preliminary problems of a political and constitutional kind would be already, by hypothesis, solved, while the problems of daily life would be passing more and more under the jurisdiction of the scientific and impartial student of definite facts. It may be prophesied, then, that the gravity of the situation created by the growth of a dissident proletariat will become less as the State is transformed into a true Republic; or, in other words that the directing and possessing classes who are not aware of the urgency of giving up their class privileges and property not justified by a functional criterion are doomed to disappear.

The *organic unanimous democracy* is the natural form which a civilized nation that has come of age must adopt. But this form can only be the last phase of a political evolution towards wisdom through liberty. The totalitarian State reached through authority and force is no more than a caricature of it. The relation to be sought between the individual and the State is one not of obedience but of perfect adaptation, and our faith consists precisely in believing that this perfect adaptation is possible if the leading classes *are* an aristocracy and if, by the virtue inherent in an aristocracy, they succeed in transforming the State into a true republic. In a State so constituted, liberty and authority will be natural functions and the political body will enjoy order, which is the collective form of health.

But where is an ideal to be found that will win the unanimity of all citizens? The dictatorial States answer: "In the nation." We are not able to accept this point of view. For us, the nation has not finality, and so is not an idea on which we could base our unanimous democracy. In our opinion the solution lies in putting frankly before the masses the humanistic ideal of organized humanity, the members of which are the nations in the service of the individual men who compose them; and in appealing to their common sense in order to find a way of adopting the best and most effective methods for the working of the collective life within each national republic. If the idea of the national republic sincerely dedicated to the service of each of its citizens and to creating the best environment for the freedom and experience of each one of them penetrates the leading classes and inspires their acts, the unanimous organic democracy will come about gradually and spontaneously and the political world will come forth from this era of struggle and discontent through

The Principles

which it is passing. For the immense majority of our ills are due to mental anarchy and its material effects. The people have no vision. Let us heal mental anarchy by offering to the people the vision of a sane humanity, ordered and organized; nothing sentimental; a practical humanity, but as great as man.

CHAPTER IV

The Natural Structure of the Nation

1. THE SOCIAL SCHEME

IN seeking a reasonable form for the State we assume that there is a "natural" or "normal" form for the nation. Communists, royalists, liberals, conservatives, whatever our political bias, trend, or school of thought, we tend to shape up our community in order to make it fit in with our idea of what it ought to be. And the question arises—whether amongst all these "ought-to-be's" which offer themselves to people's imaginations, Nature has not already made up her mind by suggesting, and even preferring, one definite form of community more in harmony than any other with her deeper laws.

If that be so, history must evince a tendency in human society to fall into such "normal" or "natural" shapes, and a glance at any familiar people or nation of Western Europe should provide us with valuable points as to nature's own ideas on this matter. As we have more than once pointed out in these pages, a constant trend of social life reproduces the same general design in all human communities. A first rough sketch of this design shows it divided into tbree tiers or layers, which go by the respective

The Natural Structure

names of people, middle class (bourgeoisie), and aristocracy.

At first sight the division of society into these three classes might be interpreted as a matter of economic and historical relationship, a chance product of time and space and other fortuitous causes. Such, in effect, is the explanation put forward by rationalists, and particularly by Marxists. But an explanation of this kind, while not altogether to be ruled out of court, must be reduced to its right limits. That economic and historical factors may account for the social pattern in three classes and, what is more to the point, for the fact that this or that individual happens to be inserted into this or that class, no one doubts. But we are not concerned with the fairness or unfairness of the fact that that human being finds himself in the skin of a peasant when he might have been a reigning price, or even a film star; what really matters is whether the division of society into three classes (with the reservations and complications anon to be studied) corresponds to some inherent law of nature, enabling us in turn to build up our political thought on a sounder basis than that of mere whim or intellectual fancy or fad.

It was, I believe, Leonardo da Vinci who said: "There are three classes of people: Those who do not see; those who see when they are shown; and those who see by themselves." This ingenious classification of human beings might provide a basis for the right understanding of the problem which we have set before us. For, if adequately interpreted, it closely fits in with the respective characteristics of the people, the bourgeoisie, and the aristocracy. A correct interpretation is, in particular, required for the word "see" in Leonardo da Vinci's dictum, which for our present purpose means "to be aware of collective life and to realize it fully and consciously."

The people in any one of our European nations is spontaneous, and its vital wealth lies in the subconscious. Its profound instinct, a depository of ancestral memories, is the psychological substratum of the whole nation. But the people's instinct is blind and insecure. Any demagogic leader will be able to draw it astray, provided he possesses magnetism, eloquence, perseverance, and what is known as a commanding personality. All that can be expected of the people is vitality, resilience, enthusiasm, a ready—but not sure—instinct for primordial and essential things. The people is, as the saying goes, a *mass*, and therefore—for mass means dough—passive and plastic. Though at times this mass be inflammable, it will not ignite of itself; the spark must come from outside, from a leader who by the mere fact that he leads ceases to belong to the people and, whatever his blood, manners, education, or political tendency, belongs, worthily or unworthily, to the aristocracy. Lenin was an aristocrat.

The social function of the people is therefore chorus-like. Individual responsibility in collective life is at its lowest in the people, and therefore the human beings who constitute it are in the best possible condition for doing as they please, for living a fully subjective life—an ideal essentially popular,

The Natural Structure

if not plebeian, which fits in admirably with the dominant feature of the people—spontaneity.

It might, at first sight, seem that in attributing to the individuals who constitute the people the best possible conditions for an unfettered subjective life we allot to them a situation of privilege. Yet subjective life does not mean personal life. The forces of impulse and instinct, which freely manifest themselves through the unfettered individual, are both beneath and beyond him, and they act through him rather than he through them, whither and wherefore he does not know. A fully subjective life is an anonymous, undifferentiated life. The individual components of the people, free to move as their instincts and impulses prompt them, are like the atoms ever stirring in the infinitesimal abysses of physical matter. They have no undifferentiated significance; their existence, their movement, their activity has no other significance than that of their aggregate transformation of energy into matter. Their energy makes the mass.

The bourgeoisie in the social design incarnates intelligence, a middle formation with an essentially executive and technical function, which consists in seeing clearly what others have discovered and carrying out accurately what others have decided. Competence and objectivity are its specific virtues. The bourgeois has no right to his place in the social design if he does not master a technique—as a tradesman, an engineer, a civil servant, a member of one of the liberal professions. Technique, on the other hand, does not allow the arbitrary individual to prevail over inert things; it exacts, on the contrary, that the individual should obey the rule of the thing in hand, for such is the only way in which the thing is to be mastered. The curing of an illness, the setting of a machine in motion, the construction of a building, require that the theory and practice of the human body, of the machine, of the art of construction should be mastered, i.e. followed and obeyed. In the social scheme the bourgeoisie is therefore the executive and conscious element; it applies the laws, carries on the everyday business of the State and of society, acts and criticizes actions; it is, in one word, the class in charge of the middle functions of the community, and, in so far as its members must be considered as pillars of the social machine, they have no right to live a fully subjective life, to do as they please, which is the popular way, since they are bound to submit to the discipline of things, and in particular to fulfil their functions rightly and to decline those functions for which they are not competent.

But the higher activities of the community are incumbent on the aristocracy. Let us save this much misused word from the untimely death which threatens it by instilling new life, i.e. new meaning into it, even though this new meaning happens to be the oldest and most accurate of all. True aristocracy has little to do with the colour of the blood. It should be meant and understood as the sum total of the men who, in a healthy community, are actually entrusted with the duties and responsibility of leadership by virtue of their inherent superiority—

The Natural Structure

those who, in the words of Leonardo da Vinci, "see by themselves," i.e. the men with the gift of creative intuition, the statesmen.

The statesman is a sculptor of peoples. He must above all possess a vision of what he wants to sculpt, in order to model the mass of his nation into this ideal shape which he wishes it to take, transfiguring it, so to speak, into its real self. The statesman, therefore, belongs less to the species of the politician than to a higher species into which are blended and transmuted that of the politician and that of the creative artist. The statesman is to the politician what the artist is to the craftsman. A Cisneros, a Richelieu, a Cortés (perhaps the greatest of the statesmen of the modern world) are nearer to the species of Bach, Shakespeare, and Leonardo da Vinci than to that of Clemenceau, Theodore Roosevelt, or Giolitti, mere men of action.

The statesman may be allowed a certain subjectivity as befits an artist. A synthesis of people and bourgeoisie, he is rich in spontaneity, though able to control and canalize it with competence and objectivity; but his supreme virtues are creative power, vision of the future, intuition of the present. These high virtues imply a certain subjectivity, a certain freedom of the self, which is, however, purified by an absolute devotion to the task, not as a result of moral discipline born of effort, but as a spontaneous gift of the self called forth by intellectual love. Above all, the statesman is naturally free from the small passions—selfishness, egotism, jealousy, vanity.

Unanimous Organic Democracy

Needless to say, such a rare human type cannot be expected to swarm in the ranks of the leading classes, even in a healthy nation. But in a healthy nation the leaders are an aristocracy, i.e. they belong to the species "statesman" just as the middle class belong to the species "expert." With greater or lesser grandeur, distinction, elegance, or even personal gifts and powers, the leaders of a healthy nation possess the specific virtues of the statesman; they assume that in their case leadership is a duty and a natural function, and they devote themselves to it with a self-denial which springs from a right intuition of the aims to be achieved, in its turn due to intellectual love.

2. THE MAN OF THE PEOPLE

The man of the people, strictly speaking, is the peasant. He lives in intimate touch with Nature, within and without. A flower sprung from the ancestral loam, he expresses with primitive purity the essence of his race in the forms of his race. The man of the people is the upholder and life-giver of the language, whose spontaneous terms and ways of speaking are prompted by the racial spirit, free from any formal influence of grammar, happily unknown rather than ignored. To know, to feel, to act, to express are in him one and the same thing. That is why popular sayings are so well rounded off, so self-contained, and lend themselves neither to analysis nor to translation. His mother-forces are instinct, memory stored up and transmitted by his

The Natural Structure

racial blood, and imagination fed by his memory. His wisdom is treasured experience.

The man of the people knows much, but not that he knows, nor what he knows, nor why he knows. His knowledge is life, and not a glance at life. Things are known just as they are lived, as experience; neither before, as foresight, nor after, as reflection. That things may be otherwise than they are is not for the man of the people a notion of experience, still less an idea, since the man of the people has no ideas. Hence his wisdom is not expressed in principles and general rules, but in stories and proverbs—symbolical forms of knowledge which carry conviction where pure reasoning could not penetrate, as all wise men and masters have ever realized. Proverbs in particular are as medals or coins of experience which circulate from hand to hand among the people.

Round and limited, these coins of experience—gold of truth in alloy with copper of cunning—the proverbs handed over from man to man and from woman to woman in a given people are inorganic and disconnected science, a heap of loose lessons on concrete but diverse facts, direct impacts of life on man and of man on life.

The life of the man of the people flows close to a native land with a taste, smell, and colour of its own which it gets from the earth and from the earth's plants and animals—the olive-tree, the vine, the cornfield, horses, mules, asses, pigs, oxen. Nature's life-rhythm such as the harvest of plants, the pregnancy and birth of animals, the moods of the sky intertwine in his experience with human life-rhythms such as the puberty of boys and girls, love and jealousy, hunger and plenty, work and sleep. The background in its simplicity has greatness and endurance; it is a background of life and death.

The man of the people knows, therefore, more definitely perhaps than the philosopher what nature is and more intimately than the physicist that there are natural laws. Animals, plants, and stars have taught him that things do not merely go down the slope of life higgledy-piggledy. But, within this wisdom, the man of the people is spontaneous. In him life wells up with the freshness of a spring, and the racial being manifests itself in full innocence. The peasant is determined by his natural environment, rooted in his land with roots, though immaterial, as sturdy as those of the oak which buries its sinewy limbs under the earth he treads. His very wisdom is born of the soil which gives it shape and flavour. And even that most universal of human emotions, religion, is in the peasant a tree of his own valley.

For what the man of the people manifests is the past, the storing up of bygone things. Just as his moods and his philosophy are the treasure of coins of experience which oral tradition has preserved for him, so even his physical gestures are the result of centuries of training and of memory. Once in Bujalance, a centre of popular artistic earthenware facing Granada, I watched a potter swiftly modelling in the clay the impeccably beautiful profile of a jar; I fancied I could see his infallible elbow guided by

The Natural Structure

whole generations of masters gone by who kept him gently within the line of perfection exacted by the standards of the place and people. And this tendency to conservatism, which in the people is identical with knowledge, since in the people nothing is known but that which is handed down and conserved, may be observed in manners, tastes, and habits. The dress, nowadays picturesque, of the peasant is but a slow local adaptation of that which, centuries earlier, was worn by courtiers. Thus the cut of the cassock and hose worn by the quechuas of the Cuzco countryside is still practically the same as that of the garments which, glittering with gold and jewels, adorned the Spanish Viceroys. Popular music is but archaic cultivated music more or less fermented under the influence of popular artists unknown even to themselves. Popular ceremonies, festivities, and customs are but reminiscences of courtly bygone days.

Normally, therefore, the man of the people is a conservative. Things, for empirical minds, can only be justified by their actual existence. How could we expect new ideas to be understood by those who have no general ideas and who live on accumulated experience? The people, therefore, provide the mass and inertia which give a healthy nation its continuity as a historical character.

To the people also is due the peculiar flavour of each national culture. The people are like the earth in which the stubble and the residues of the harvest and the refuse of the farm are buried and rot, so that their fertile fermentation may go to enrich and vivify the seed of future crops. From their unfathomable vitality spring the masters who now and then come to renew and refresh other social layers exhausted by their conscious work—for nothing exhausts like conscious work. From their long, leisurely glances, which have drunk numberless scenes and colours in apparent passivity and silence, spring, in the course of time, the Titians and the Goyas who give them back in glorious pictures to immortality.

But, so that the deep layers of the nation remain fertile, it is indispensable that their life be respected in its depth, that is, that the side of the nation should not be stabbed, bringing out into the light of exhausting and desiccating consciousness the rich and generous blood which, if allowed to circulate in obscure hiding within its veins and arteries, will feed its brain for ever, and for ever make its heart beat in health and strength.

3. THE BOURGEOIS

Considered in its essential depth and not merely in its social façade, the bourgeoisie may be described as the class of men who, without intuition to discover things, possess a clear intelligence which understands them once discovered, and a technique which masters them and puts them to a social use.

The bourgeois therefore implies a state of things, an *order*, within which he is an important, if not the pivotal, element. While the people are the depository of the past, while the aristocrat (in our sense of the

The Natural Structure

word) is the forerunner of the future, the bourgeois is the living consciousness of the present. To be conscious of the present is to possess a *culture*. The bourgeois is therefore the social prototype and the protagonist of an existing culture. If he has no culture, a man is not a bourgeois.

And to begin with, a technical culture. The bourgeois does not fulfil his social functions if he does not master one given order of things—commercial, industrial, administrative, scientific, educational, professional. Whatever the walk of life he has chosen, it is his duty to know it inherently and, so to say, in an original way, not merely by hearsay, or on trust from books or other people. For the basis of the bourgeoisie is professional usefulness. Through his profession the bourgeois handles and turns to account the capital of ideas and discoveries which circulate in the state of things within which he is inserted. No one asks him to invent, discover, explore; but he is expected to know, to be informed, to realize what is going on, to be useful in some concrete way, to be reliable and to inspire confidence in his capacity, in his competence, and in his straightforwardness. If he is not useful, he is not a bourgeois.

Yet his social function is by no means limited to his technical capacity and usefulness. His culture must be general as well as technical. There is a first reason for this, arising out of his purely technical requirements and obligations: in order fully to master any profession it is necessary to visualize it within the social framework in which it is inserted, so that the man who deliberately clips off all other interests but the strictly professional is not merely a bore and an inhuman piece of machinery, but falls short of professional standards as well. He who is "nothing but" is "not even."

Moreover, beyond his professional duty the bourgeois has also to fulfil the wider social obligation of upholding and developing a collective culture. Since in the social scheme the bourgeoisie stands for intelligence, the bourgeois must give full scope to this important human faculty; he must try to understand what is happening, i.e. to create and to represent the collective consciousness of the existing order of things. From this general principle the primary duties of all bourgeois may be deducted.

The first of them is *objectivity*. To understand is to see, and to see implies a minimum of respect towards what one sees. The bourgeois must therefore shun all arbitrariness. As a social type he is not called upon to strike new paths of originality, but to keep straight on the royal road of standards. He should control and discipline his imagination, an essentially popular faculty, useful and even fruitful in the people, dangerous in the bourgeois. To this end he should be well informed. Curiosity, both technical and general, is one of the duties of the bourgeois as well as one of his rights, on which, by the way, the principle of liberty of thought (hence of the Press) may well be established.

With objectivity the bourgeois must possess *measure*—an essentially intellectual quality, for to

The Natural Structure

think is to weigh and to weigh is to measure. The bourgeois must be measured in his words and opinions and watch himself so as not to permit waves of passion or the fever of mental activity to run over or impair his permanent thought. It follows that the discipline and measure, which are intellectual conditions for his thought, must also command the life of his passion and emotions, actions, habits, and even gestures. For one who measures seeks a balance, and how could he find a balance in things if he has not found it in his own self?

That is why we expect of the bourgeois a certain reserve, a certain good form in his way of living. *Good form* is a revealing expression. For form is an intellectual attribute, the result of understanding, of being aware of things. In the community the bourgeois must be the upholder of form in ideas and in manners. Form is no trifling, no superficial affair. It is the façade of stability, for nothing which is not stable can have form. Smoke, clouds, flowing water have no form. Woe to the nation whose bourgeoisie underestimates, neglects, or obliterates social forms.

For it behoves the bourgeois to keep up clear forms for ethical habits, social rites, critical rules, and aesthetic standards. Such is in particular the main utility of what is called "hospitality." The host and hostess are priests of a most important social rite. The table, the reception rooms are places of culture consumption: they are social culture actually lived, for in them all the arts are blended with the most difficult of them—the art of living,

Unanimous Organic Democracy

In the bourgeois' home, open and hospitable, organized for this social function, the collective forms of living are asserted, developed, and refined. The social rites of dress are one of the most significant signs of culture. A nation which neglects them may be disguising under the attractive pretext of democratic simplicity mere slovenliness, a lazy lack of social discipline. There is a pathetic story of the Napoleonic epic which illustrates this value of dress as a social rite. During one of the most desolate phases of the disastrous retreat from Moscow, when the Grand Army melted away in the endless plains of Russia, a brigadier-general sought an audience with the Emperor. When he was introduced into the presence of Napoleon, the Emperor found before him a spick-and-span figure, clean-shaved, spotless, as if the audience were taking place at the Tuileries. With tears in his eyes the Emperor shook hands with him: "General, you are an honest man." There is a virtue, if not in dress, in the discipline which makes of it a social rite.

The most important rule of the bourgeois is to be a consumer of culture. A work of art is but a manifestation, i.e. a potential transmission, of spirit. It cannot be said to have achieved its purpose until the consumer of art has enjoyed it. The pictures of Titian, the chapters of Don Quixote, the scenes of Shakespeare, the melodies of Mozart are as bows open and taut, constantly waiting for the human being through whose soul their tension may be closed and resolved. Taste for the bourgeois is a social duty. His home, his whole life must tend

The Natural Structure

towards the highest possible level of his time in intellectual, moral, and aesthetic values. The social duty of taste implies the social duty of criticism. In professional, as well as in general matters, the bourgeois is the trustee of the cultural patrimony of the nation; he is the keeper of standards.

It follows that the bourgeois must be conservative. Since he is intelligent and has general ideas, he is a liberal conservative, open to change, but conscious of the value of his inherited estate. Being measured and objective, he is not prone to revolution.

4. THE ARISTOCRAT

I mean by *aristocrat* the man who, in matters of collective life, sees by himself; who realizes what is going on in all its depth, and is able to detect the seeds of the future in the recesses of the present; who can conceive the image of what collective reality ought to become in a desirable future, actually wishes such a future to materialize, and devotes himself to the task of bringing it about and of shaping his world to fit the image of his vision, animated by the highest of all passions—intellectual love.

No one appoints, elects or chooses the aristocrat. He knows himself to be one because he hears himself called to his high and arduous endeavour by an internal voice—his vocation. There is no voice with more commanding power; none which can obtain more punctual and loyal obedience. Chief and soldier within one soul, under one will, within the same executive body, the aristocrat obeys his vocation without any possible excuse or evasion. He is his own slave.

For the first duty of the aristocrat is to master himself. Discipline is the first law of his life. Actions, thoughts, and words must in him submit to the leadership of the higher faculties. Farewell to "I do as I please." The whims and promptings hidden under "I please" are obscure forces roaming in the ancestral bush, a kind of dragon which the aristocrat must master and tame. His driving impulse well in hand, his virile energy disciplined to action, his tongue controlled by his thought, and his thought at the service of his high endeavour, the aristocrat is, in short, a man who has attained a degree of complete consciousness and responsibility.

He owns himself in order to give himself. His vocation dictates to him his task. His intellectual love makes him a slave of it. The aristocrat asks nothing for himself—but all that is necessary for his work. And as his work is arduous, it exacts more and more devotion from him. The aristocrat rises in an ascending scale of duties. At every step his path becomes narrower and steeper. Hence, though the profession be open, there is no surplus, but rather a lack, of aristocrats. The only privilege of the aristocrat is to have more duties than the rest of the citizens—duties which he cannot evade, for he is his own police, judge, and executioner.

The aristocrat fights on two fronts: that of outward reality, which he endeavours to model and shape so as to fit his own inner vision, and which revolts and bites his hands; and the front of inward reality,

The Natural Structure

where he meets the weak and frail man within, the man of the people who in his own soul resists him because he wants to do as he pleases, and the bourgeois who in his own soul settles down and seeks to enjoy in selfishness every available comfort and privilege. The life of the aristocrat knows no rest. Taut as a sonorous string, the work pulls at him, he pulls at the work.

The relation between the aristocrat and his self is thus delicate and complex. Like everything in him, this relation is determined by the supreme law of his existence, which is devotion to his work. The aristocrat subordinates his person to his work. His duties clearly follow this rule; self-denial, but not self-negation. The aristocrat has the right to ask and the duty to demand all that he needs as a tool for his work. Nothing less, but nothing more. Nothing more, but nothing less. He knows, moreover, that the less he requires, even on the instrumental plane where he has the right and the duty to ask, the more effective he will be.

He should not expect popularity. He may obtain it. He may not. There is no certain relation between good service and popularity. He should therefore put aside all fear of incurring unpopularity, or even the anger of the people. Within a more restrained circle he may come to feel the sour breath of envy. But the aristocrat cannot afford to let himself be influenced by his surroundings. He must receive his experiences as data to stimulate his mind, never as blows to rouse his emotions. Just as our eyes respond to everything, even to physical blows, by giving back sensations of light, so the soul of the aristocrat transfigures even the blows of destiny into the light of comprehension and knowledge.

To the lower passions usually called forth by collective life—disillusion, vindictiveness, spite, wounded pride—he can oppose two natural advantages: one innate, the other one developed. Since he sees by himself, since he realizes what is going on, he accepts all that happens to him with the same equanimity wherewith he accepts the rain, good and bad weather, a storm; and since he has learnt the value of discipline, he does not allow his own personal reactions to cloud his thought or to warp his action.

Serenity is therefore the main virtue of the aristocrat—innate, since he sees, and only in mental darkness can man lose his serenity; cultivated, for moral discipline will watch over actions and reactions so that they do not lead the mind astray from the luminous poise which is the essence of serenity.

This virtue rests on three staunch pillars; one is the clear vision of surrounding reality in its past, its present, and its possible future; and so that the whole curve of its development fits in with a general conception of life; the second is absolute self-denial; and the third is the conviction that, in the end, the world is not ours, and everyone, from the humblest craftsman to the highest artist, everyone is the instrument of higher designs. The aristocrat knows that his responsibility ceases with his self-denial. He serves, and that is all he is required to do. Both in and out of his work, he gives himself up to it without

The Natural Structure

stint; but he is not troubled in his soul by the possibility of failure. Over the furrow which will cover his bones the same sun will ripen other harvests.

5. THE WORKMAN

The workman is a social type which stands between the man of the people and the bourgeois. His popular origin is recent, but the evolution which leads him away from the people may be more or less advanced according to circumstances of place and craft. The village smiths or carpenters, who devote most of their work to the making or repairing of the peasants' tools, who belong to peasant families and live peasants' lives, are men of the people almost intact. The gardener, who even in the town works amongst plants, bent over the breath of Mother Earth, is perhaps the most "man-of-the-people" amongst urban workmen. But the most discriminating factor as between workman and workman is technique. Skilled workers and unskilled workers, much as politics may endeavour to unite them, are separate social types. The workman who masters a craft thoroughly acquires not only control over a set of things and actions—electricity, water, steam, wood—but a certain self-reliance and a kind of dignity which assimilate him to the bourgeois. Thus, in healthy countries, the skilled worker tends towards the bourgeois type and takes on the features of the bourgeoisie, particularly the tendency to stable conditions and to the cultivation of mind and taste. Such bourgeois inner promptings do not go without outward signs, as, for instance, in the manner of dress. Since—whether revolutionists like it or not—culture is mostly a bourgeois form of life, dress is dictated to all classes by the bourgeois. So that, as soon as the skilled workman realizes his superiority over the unskilled man, he expresses it in such signs as a collar, a necktie, a coat, and a hat. All observers of Soviet Russia have underlined the significance of the resurrection of the necktie amongst the rising Bolshevik élite.

The skilled worker is thus one of the poles of what is most inaccurately described as the working class, an inaccuracy which afflicts both the substantive *class*, for they are not a class, and the qualification *working*, for they do not *all* work. At the other pole we find what in our opinion constitutes the true *proletariat*, i.e. a mixed mass composed mostly of unskilled workers, and also of workers trained for skilled trades who have not made good owing to lack of ability or character. This mass of people without roots, without a definite social function or class, is like a social steppe covered with a sterile and dry vegetation ready to take fire.

It may be worth observing, by the way, that the proletarian thus understood, i.e. the inefficient and unskilled worker at the mercy of events, is not without parallel types in the other layers of society: in the people, the tramp; in the middle classes, the hanger-on, good-for-nothing, Mr. Micawber sort of person; in the aristocracy, the young man about town, the bohemian artist, the futile intellectual or

The Natural Structure

aesthete; human beings whose life floats away, tossed here and there by collective ebbs and eddies, between laziness and vanity.

The workman is then a somewhat undefined social type which wavers between three well-defined ones; the man of the people, the bourgeois, the "proletarian." For in fact the workman fulfils no specific social function; he is not a natural social type. This does not of course mean that workmen, in the plural, as separate individuals not put together into a social class, are not definite social beings, with concrete social functions; but merely that there is no such thing as a "working class" in the same way as there are popular, bourgeois, and aristocratic classes. Note the curious paradox: it is precisely the kind of people amongst whom the disastrous doctrine of class struggle finds readiest adepts, the kind of people who, through insistent emotional propaganda, have been made to feel themselves as "the working class," who in the community are the least apt to form one. A social zone of ill-defined outlines, they are conterminous with the bourgeoisie, the people, and the proletariat; they overlap and, up to a point, intermix with these three other social zones, but lack a class unit of their own.

It is obvious that this paradox carries within its very terms its own solution. Gravitation implies attraction. There are always in a workman one—at times there are two—of these three possible attractions. Either he feels drawn up towards the bourgeoisie, or he lets himself go down the fatal slope leading towards the proletariat, or he remains closely attached to the warm popular countryside. And just because the working "class" carries within it this inevitable tendency towards disintegration, the class-struggle myth, on the basis of the proletariat, which is not the working class but its failure, has been invented and is angrily raised before the workers in order to stimulate the collective consciousness of a class which, of its own accord, refuses to exist.

In such observations, by the way, one explanation may be found for a number of facts of contemporary material life, for instance the absence of unemployment in Soviet Russia. Such a boon is only enjoyed by skilled workers, i.e. workers with a bourgeois tendency. Through the operation of a natural law, a bourgeoisie is gradually emerging from the masses so energetically and ruthlessly equalized in the first glow of Marxist enthusiasm. Skilled workers and the liberal professions compose it, just as in so-called capitalistic nations, and just as in them the proletariat (in our sense of the word, the unskilled masses) suffer from unemployment. Again in England, revolutionary extremist socialism is practically unknown; this may be partly due to temperamental causes, as shown by the fact that in Great Britain most of the exponents of extremism hail from Scotland; but it is surely due also to the abundance of skilled workers whose proclivities are naturally bourgeois and who dislike the very word revolution. As a contrast, extremist views are to be found in countries but poorly industrialized, because in such countries skilled workers are in a minority,

The Natural Structure

while there abounds in them a turbulent mass of unskilled workers without roots, stability, technique, stake in the land; a mass ready to receive Messianic messages and over-simplified visions of paradise on earth and of socialism in our day.

On this social zone, open towards three other fields, the written letter exerts a disturbing influence, while the silent suggestions of patient Mother Earth no longer act. The workman is already uprooted from land tradition, not yet rooted into culture. He is therefore tossed to and fro, not merely between three social classes, but between three cultures; a natural earth-culture where he has no root; and a conscious mental culture which he has not yet acquired. It is both unfair and inhuman to expect that, over and above the overwhelming responsibility of the struggle for a salary, he should take on those of a self-education which other social types more fortunately placed cannot shoulder unaided. Nothing then more natural than his frequent surrender to the sirens of dogmatism.

His threefold gravitation determines his final reaction towards social-political problems. The skilled worker, who controls a craft, who is respected in his trade, gravitates towards the bourgeois type; he is moderate in his judgments and opinions about industrial relations and public affairs, for he realizes that the problems which they suggest are complex, and he is cautious about a so-called ideal which would make him the equal, and therefore the dupe, of the incompetent and slothful worker. The peasant worker feels in his blood the weight of tradition.

Unanimous Organic Democracy

The "proletarian" is often an extremist who seeks the transformation of society seen as an abstraction; for, severed from the land which had given a sense of concrete things to his ancestors, he feeds his mind on printed stuff. For him life is not a valley of known shape and colour, with familiar springs, paths, trees, and animals, closed by a row of hills, behind which hides and stretches the wide world; but a set of general and abstract ideas definitely positive or negative such as "society," "capitalism," "labour," a mechanical outlook in which ideas take on the hard-and-fast shape of pieces of machinery.

And thus it is that the "working class," which, in the normal constitution of a healthy country, has no natural place as a class, comes forward as a protagonist to the first line of collective problems; for in it may be seen at work, and often in utter confusion, three kinds of gravitation: a bourgeois, liberal-conservative tendency, due to intelligence and craftsmanship; a peasant conservative tendency, due to tradition and instinct; and a proletarian, revolutionary tendency, due to uprooting and dire need.

6. OTHER SOCIAL TYPES

Here is then our social scheme with its three tiers: aristocracy, bourgeois, people, and a mass of workers gravitating towards the bourgeois, towards the people, or towards a kind of repository of nondescript human beings for which we reserve the name of proletariat. But there are ever so many human types which do not fit into any of these classes; there is the grocer.

The Natural Structure

the artist, the idle landlord, the swindler, the adventurer. Life cannot be expected meekly to submit to our geometrical forms. Though it tend to adopt the three-class shape, it by no means limits its creative power to them, but keeps overflowing our social moulds with all kinds of other forms and oddities. Yet these somewhat exceptional forms lack the constancy to remain true to type, without which a regular social class cannot be evolved, and therefore tend to gravitate to one or other of the three permanent classes with a life of their own.

All these extra-types may be reduced to two, according to whether the predominant element in them be a creative virtue, which is an upward force, or an inert mass, which will fatally draw them downwards. The human types which make up the first category, precisely because they are endowed with life and vigour, tend to differentiate and clearly gravitate towards one or other of the three social classes. The human types which make up the second category, precisely because in them the predominant element is an inert mass without enough vital spirit to keep it at its original social level, fall continuously, and as they fall lose all volume, specific features, and differentiation; they sink thus into the amorphous, undefined, and depressed mass of the proletariat (in the sense here given to this word, by no means to be understood as synonymous with "working class").

Thus, for instance, the retailer is a kind of bourgeois. He is not yet one because he lacks a certain number of bourgeois features; his technique or craft is by no means negligible, for he is a distributor, and therefore is entrusted with an important social function, for on its being well fulfilled with the minimum of expense and of waste of energy hangs considerable advantage to the nation. And yet it is obvious that, through one of the many imponderabilia which exert so much influence on human life, the craft of the retailer lacks social prestige. Moreover, even in a healthy nation the retailer usually lacks the necessary social and mental culture to fulfil the all-round function of a bourgeois. And yet the bourgeois is the type toward which he tends, the model of his ambitious aims, which he often realizes, if not in his own person, in that of his children.

Artists, taken as a whole, gravitate towards the aristocracy in the sense which we attach to this word. They are men endowed with a creative intuition whose life is, or ought to be, a kind of permanent devotion and self-denial in the service of their own creative gift. Yet it goes without saying that there are amongst them weaker brethren who, far from living up to the standards of the Order—for Art is an Order, and a severe one—gravitate towards the bourgeoisie by the way of commercialism, or else, lacking inspiration, moral discipline, or both, fall gradually towards the proletariat by the pleasant slopes of bohemianism.

Big landlords—persons who by tradition, luck, or competence wield considerable social power—are also a kind of aristocracy. In the idea of the community the aristocrat is the man who considers it

The Natural Structure

as his duty to serve the commonwealth for the sake of the commonwealth without any other outward obligation to do so. To a greater or lesser extent we may therefore consider as aristocrats—good or bad ones—those who, by vocation or situation, have to deal with the general good, or with enterprises so vast that they noticeably influence the general good.

Thus a big rural landlord who understands his privileged situation as an opportunity for taking on the duties of leadership for the benefit, general welfare, and progress of the particular district over which he happens to wield power, who raises the value of the land by appropriate means, who improves the local schools, the municipal administration, the housing of the peasants; who, in short, takes on local government at the cost of his own leisure and possibly of his direct material interests—is a successful aristocrat; while the landlord who limits his activities to the choosing of a manager, taking as the best the one who brings him the biggest rent with the least amount of trouble, is a failure as an aristocrat.

Then again, the financier who devotes his life talent to making the capital he controls as creative as possible at the cheapest cost to the nation is a successful aristocrat; if he is content to pile up fees upon fees, understanding his rôle as that of a highly efficient super-leech, he is a failure as an aristocrat.

The nobleman, heir to a great name, who makes of his house and wealth a centre of irradiation of social, intellectual, and artistic culture, is a successful aristocrat; but if all he does is to live in comfortable frivolity, he is a failure as an aristocrat.

Thus the social scheme stands out before our eyes in all its complexity, yet on the whole clear. The main lines of its structure suggest three tiers: the people, made up of peasants, rooted in the earth and devoted to it, steeped in that traditional wisdom which is like the flavour of life itself, constitute the repository of the past; the bourgeoisie, the class which stands for technique, intelligence, order, and culture, represents the state of things and the present; and the aristocracy, a small but creative group of men gifted with vision and self-denial, see the future and prepare its advent with their disinterested activity. Round these three natural orders of society other less definite groups, great or small, may be discerned, whose component individuals gravitate towards one or other of the natural orders; the working man, skilled and sure in his skill, tends towards the bourgeoisie; the great landlords and noblemen, if they happen to possess an inherent virtue in proportion to their responsibilities, gravitate towards the aristocracy; and right through society the lazy, the poor in spirit or in body, the feeble, the weak, fatally fall towards the "proletariat."

7. BUT MUST IT BE?

Now it may be argued, granted that such a division of our society into people, bourgeoisie, and aristocracy, with the attendant undefined groups which gravitate to one or other of them, be the natural

The Natural Structure

structure of our society, why should we resign ourselves to it? Is not all civilization an effort away from nature, precisely a victory over nature? Had we accepted nature's ways in every form of life, we should still be eating raw meat, possibly that of our enemies and elderly relations; raping women; living the life of a featherless biped. Progress consists precisely in our constant endeavour to raise human life to its highest possible level. Nothing is therefore proved by showing that this tripartite form of society has been spontaneously adopted by all human communities, for the mind will always claim its right to devise a higher form than the mere prompting of human nature.

This objection is substantial and stands at the basis of the communistic theory of the classless state. We could not proceed further without dealing with it. That the threefold scheme of society is natural there is no doubt. Such a persistence in itself should inspire some respect in us, for it would appear to suggest the existence of natural laws which determine collective evolution towards the same stable equilibrium. Yet the objection stands. In human affairs natural facts must justify themselves inherently, and not merely as being natural. Cruelty is as natural as mercy, crime as natural as justice.

Let us then justify our social scheme on its own merits. There is, to begin with, a significant correspondence between its three main classes and the three main forms of human knowledge: imagination-memory, intelligence, intuition.

Unanimous Organic Democracy

Imagination-memory is the primitive, spontaneous, and subconscious form of knowledge. It springs from the unfathomable depths of the earth, the human blood, the ancestral magma. Through his imagination-memory man is connected with his remotest racial past, and receives from it the experience accumulated by many an ancestral life, lived images deeply impressed in the recesses of the individual who lived them, handed down from generation to generation along with the gesture, the voice, and the elusive, mysterious, and all-pervading likeness. The imagination-memory is therefore a collective form of knowledge. It has but little individuality, and it comes out most vigorously in children and in uncultivated persons, precisely when the individual personality is too vague and undelineated to hinder its communal promptings.

Intelligence is the conscious form of knowledge. By means of his intelligence the individual, through a deliberate and active movement of his differentiated being, "seizes" things and appropriates them. Most of the words which describe a *successful* mental operation are borrowed from the vocabulary of physical grasping. To *grasp*, to *seize*, to *apprehend*, to *comprehend*, and last but not least to *assimilate*, suggest the same idea of acquisition and appropriation by positive—one might almost say aggressive—action, wherein the work of the human mind on outside objects consists. The mind is therefore the manager and the administrator of the power which man wields over things, thanks to his capacity for realizing the laws that rule them. Man does not reach the

The Natural Structure

stage of complete mental power until he is grown up and unless his conscious personality is fully developed; because the mind is an individual faculty since it implies attention controlled by a well-defined will.

And then, over and above intelligence, there is another form of knowledge, swifter and more complete, a super-conscious knowledge, which we call intuition. Just as through imagination-memory man is able to know all that surges in him from the depths of his ancestral blood; just as through his conscious intelligence he knows all that which he himself can *seize* by an effort of his will; so, by means of intuition, he perceives in a kind of revelation the direct light of reality. Intuition is a gift which grows with age, as experience weakens the faith in mere intellect. While imagination-memory is a pre-individual, and intelligence an individual, faculty, intuition is a post-individual gift. And marvellous and even paradoxical as it may sound, it happens that the first and the last, the two un-individual sources of knowledge, manifest themselves in concrete ways and through strictly personal and often intransferable experiences which we call *remembrances, images, inklings, visions*; while the intellect, the essentially individual faculty, gives forth general ideas, perfectly interchangeable and bearing no special mark from the person who first utters them.

Now it is significant that the three fundamental and natural classes of the State correspond to these three sources of knowledge in the human being.

Unanimous Organic Democracy

The people incarnate the imagination-memory of the nation; the bourgeoisie, the conscious intellect; the aristocracy, creative intuition. And a nation is the healthier, and therefore the happier, the more the actual social classes correspond to the natural classes thus defined in terms of psychical life.

The notion of the classless State—whatever the arguments for or against it on the economic plane—is an obvious psychological aberration due to the curious incomprehension for spiritual things which afflicts the mere intellect. "Ils n'ont que raison," said de Maistre. The intellectuals look down on the merely imaginative man. Hence the romantic attitude about "liberating" the peasant with "books," "the lights of learning," and "schools." Not for a moment does it occur to them that there are several human types, and that it is good that it should be so: not for a moment do they wonder whether on balance both the individual concerned and the nation would not be better off if many a peasant remained unlettered rather than be turned into a reader of the *Daily Error*; not for a moment do they surmise that the "personal" acquaintance with a concrete and individual olive-tree, with its peculiar twists, wrinkles and hollows, habits, tendencies and vices, is as valuable in its way as the abstract notion of the olive-tree, the tree of Minerva, of such a species and genus according to Linnaeus. The idea of reducing to one single plane all the psychical wealth which our modern societies contain is therefore a purely intellectualistic conception and reveals an insufficient grasp of both imagination and

The Natural Structure

intuition. Not in vain does it hail from a Jewish thinker, i.e. a man belonging to a race which for many centuries has lived without roots, and therefore without a "people."

The Jews are not the only nation without a "people," i.e. without that section of the nation which, being in closer touch with the earth than the rest, is particularly fitted to express and to incarnate the imagination-memory of the community. Most, if not all, of the nations of the American Continent are nations without a people, or else with a people lacking one or other of the conditions favourable for a strong and rich imagination-memory: either the density of the population is too thin; or the settling too recent; or the origin of the peasantry too varied and the blend too superficial. The psychical and social phenomena which spring from such a fact would repay study. In the South American States we would point out as one of the most important of them the strong Indian attitude often adopted even by white South Americans when the nation has a numerous Indian population; in the United States the higher level of genuine human culture attained by states such as New England, where a relatively steady and old peasantry exists; as well as the undoubted influence of the negro imagination-memory on the culture of the Southern States.

It would appear therefore that the three-tier structure which societies tend to adopt is not merely the outcome of social-economic laws, which the mind is free to combat and amend; but also the manifestation of a deep psychical reality in harmony with the inner constitution of the individual being.

8. THE HEALTHY NATION

A healthy nation is a nation which wants to persevere in its own being. A nation has no separate existence from the individuals who compose it—it only exists in so far as it exists in them. It follows that a nation is healthy if the individuals who compose it are aware of its existence and wish effectively that this existence subsist; if they wish it, not as a mere volition with more or less intermittent effects, but as a permanent attitude of the will which may be relied upon at every challenge of experience.

This attitude of mind implies that the individual is aware of the *organic nature of the nation*. Nations are strong when the particular person feels in him the living sense of the general; when the individual realizes that the nation is a complex being, not a mere sum total of "inhabitants" nor a battlefield for civil wars. Hence it is that in healthy nations there is everywhere a high feeling of unity, which brings the whole nation home to every one of the groups within it.

This is then a first feature of healthy nations, which sets them apart from sick ones; the sense of the organic character of the community. In them political parties, for instance, even though they may be opposed in their ideas, have more in common than in opposition, like two brothers who resemble

The Natural Structure

each other more than they differ from each other; while in sick nations political parties feel nothing in common. And this advantage of unity over diversity is in healthy countries a constant feature to be observed at every stage in the division and subdivision of the nation's tree of life, so that whatever point of the life of the community we may choose to observe, we shall see unanimity prevail over divergence and solidarity over incompatibility.

For in a healthy nation the social evolution which determines the divisions and subdivisions within the country's life springs from the *real* and not from the *personal* pole of happenings, or, in other words, social groups are divided and subdivided not because a particular individual requires it so, but because things in themselves demand it. As it is evident that things in themselves arising in the life of the nation cannot of their own accord demand the disintegration of the nation, since they are in their nature organic parts of the national whole, it follows that in the groups and sub-groups which are created in a healthy country in order to serve real needs the sense of unity of the nation always overrides that of the division which separates group from group.

Needless to say, this observation does not apply merely to the political field, which national life greatly exceeds. All groups within the collective being—universities, clubs, commercial firms, government departments, pleasure or business undertakings—all the communities of any kind which go to the making of the national whole in a healthy nation reveal this tendency to make the sense of the unity of the group prevail over that of the variety of its components, and the sense of the unity of the nation over that of the variety of the groups.

Such is the first natural virtue which flows from the sense of organic life in healthy nations. Healthy nations know that they *are*. But, moreover, they want to persevere in their being. And this second virtue leads them to create in their midst the organs which they need, not only to live, but to live well. A healthy nation, in order to live well, must possess an aristocracy to guide and organize it and a bourgeoisie to administer it. When the nation is healthy it gives forth such a bourgeoisie and such an aristocracy. A healthy nation manifests its capacity to create a bourgeoisie by spontaneously producing generations of youth wishing to acquire genuine knowledge. A careful observation of students in a nation provides a criterion of its health. If the student seeks but a mere diploma which without knowledge may enable him to steal into the comfortable harbours of the country's bureaucracy, the nation is sick; it mistakes an illusion for a reality; it believes that the bourgeoisie is a class of men who wear neckties and can employ two domestic servants; if the student seeks truly and effectively to master a technique, the nation is healthy; it knows that the bourgeoisie is a class of competent experts, capable of dealing with the problems arising out of the physical and moral health, the education, the economy, and the culture of the community. For, in either case, the students are but answering to the tacit demand of the country.

The Natural Structure

But the healthy nation knows also how to give forth an aristocracy, i.e. a class of men who see it consciously as it is and as it should be, whose ambition it is to lead the nation towards this better image of itself which they contemplate. A nation therefore lives fully only in its aristocracy, and it might be said no nation really exists fully unless it has given forth an aristocracy. The aristocratic virtue flowing throughout the national body quickens the bourgeoisie and the people. In its purest meaning, patriotism is an aristocratic virtue. *Patrician* means father of the country. The omnipresence, in a greater or lesser degree, throughout the nation, of an aristocratic spirit, i.e. of the organic sense of the community stimulated by intellectual love for the vision of a better country to be, provides that first impulse which raises the leader above the level of those who surround him. In the healthy nation this initial rise, wholly natural and spontaneous, calls forth a favourable reaction which stimulates the coming leader and encourages him to take on more duties, a sure way of rising higher. The trust of his countrymen, their affection, later on their admiration, and the support of his followers create a favourable "climate" for his inherent aristocratic tendency, and make of him an aristocrat. In sick nations this rise of the leader calls forth the envy of those who lack his inherent forces; they do not see the duties that he voluntarily assumes, but the external advantages, possibly the miserable material gain involved, perhaps the pleasures of a wider range of commandment, interpreted with low simplicity as a wider range for a "do as I please." And the rising leader falls back discouraged to the ranks, or else fights on his way up the slopes of responsibility in growing solitude and hostility. Thus in sick nations the aristocracy is thin, sparse, and disheartened.

Obviously, if the organic sense of the healthy nation implies the prevalence of unity over variety, it is sure to manifest itself in the discipline of the citizen before the social whole. At every step in the collective hierarchy service will prevail over the servant, things over persons. This will therefore be yet another of the symptoms of health in a nation: its conscious citizens are aware that the nation can only exist and subsist if the citizen is subordinated to his task, and his task to the nation.

9. SPONTANEOUS ORGANIZATION

Stars, crystals, mirrors, clear surfaces, rays of light, geometric orbits, infallible eclipses, ether waves vibrating in space with mathematical exactitude; all that harmony, as free and spontaneous, but as precise and sure, as a fugue of Bach, which is, in the universe, the manifestation of divine intelligence, marvellous though it be, though it leave the mind in suspense, does not overwhelm it as does the unswerving instinct of the humble cell which, in the dark recesses of an animal or plant, moulds the details of life with a full understanding of its whole body.

Marvel of marvels. The human germ carries within its minute compass, and within its seemingly

The Natural Structure

elementary constitution, the integral image of the whole adult body, incomparably bigger and more complex. For if it did not hold within itself, in some ways unfathomable to us, the image of the whole being to be, how could it gradually evolve such being without any other outer help than the pure material-energetic help of food, so that at any moment in the process the whole that is, constitutes an organism fit for the present and potentially fit for the future.

When the foetus is well under way some of its cells are, for instance, specialized in the development of the heart, or of parts thereof. These cells, however humble and obscure the corner of the heart *towards* which they are working, must possess the image of that particular corner, and of the whole heart, and even of the whole body, since the heart without the whole body has no sense. Therefore the marvel of life lies in this special virtue that its parts spontaneously organize themselves towards a total prototype, the image of which pre-exists as a whole in all the parts which work towards it; or, in other words, that the whole is present in all its parts as an animating principle.

Such a virtue is also observable in a healthy community. The vitality of a nation may be measured in terms of its capacity for spontaneous organization. While the organs of the State, what might be described as its framework and skeleton, grow in most cases from the central nucleus of royal authority, the organs of a nation in a healthy country grow spontaneously from local groups which, animated by a synthetic sense of the nation, coalesce and harmonize with each other until they gradually grow into a kind of muscular tissue of the whole nation, covering the skeleton of the mere State.

As this virtue has been observed to flourish in England with particular vigour, it is known all over the world by the English name of "Self-Government." There was a time when it was strong in Spain also, a fact which explains, by the way, why the conquest of America should have struck root so quickly and deeply; for the real conquest of America was due not so much to the conquistadors as to the *cabildos* which they founded as soon as the battle was over.

The prejudices evolved during the nineteenth century as a result of the French Revolution, based on the half-arithmetical, half-mystical notion of "the people," sometimes lend to self-government a democratic colour. A pure anachronism, for self-government is, both in time and in the permanent hierarchy of the spirit, previous to and more primitive than the self-conscious idea of democracy. Self-government is neither democratic nor aristocratic. It is merely spontaneous and organic. If closely watched in concrete examples, it will be found to evince a happy tendency to harmonize in one living whole the acquiescence of the many, the collaboration of the few, and the initiative of the One, i.e. in every case what might be described as a "cell of self-government" will be found to consist of a *leader* surrounded by *competent men* acting on *people*; or, in terms of our own vocabulary, an *aristocrat* surrounded

The Natural Structure

by a group of *bourgeois* working with the *people* for the benefit of the nation. The virtue of self-government is therefore merely the capacity for spontaneously creating such cells—a capacity which out of the mass makes a nation; it is as impartial and indifferent to the issues of Democracy and Aristocracy as is the phenomenon known as Life, which from mere matter makes a body.

Needless to say, spontaneous organization is not to be understood as a merely political virtue. Politics after all is but the surface, or at most one of the forms of collective life. Thus, for instance, a spontaneous organization of professions, endowed with an organic national sense, leads to an admirable wealth of collective life, since it puts at the disposal of the whole nation professional associations which add the advantage of co-ordination to that of competence. When the spirit of spontaneous organization animates a nation it instils life into all the channels of the community. Not only does it raise the level of efficiency of the State institutions; not only does it bring forth professional associations which collaborate freely in the work of the State; but it creates within the community groups of devoted activities in the service of culture, charity, health, justice, all the values which go to the making of a national civilization, and thus secures fulfilment of numerous collective functions without calling on State help. The State saves in this way much expense and much energy. Inspection is easy or needless, since the national spirit which gives rise to these groups and keeps them alive suffices to ensure a satisfactory

Unanimous Organic Democracy

working of them. And even individual lives thus enlisted in a concrete service and disciplined into a co-operative activity find themselves justified and balanced, happy to feel consumed in a luminous way, just as the tallow of the candle is ennobled by passing into flame and light.

The law allows all that it does not forbid. It permits therefore all citizens to gather themselves into associations for the service of the world. The spirit of spontaneous organization may or may not animate these associations of citizens. In strong nations vitality may be observed at all levels and in all nooks and corners of the community, in that individuals are organized into cells polarized towards the common good. In weak nations the individual remains isolated and inert, unless he consumes his surplus energy in pointless agitation, and therefore in raising an unhealthy fever in the national body. The difference is obvious between the two situations, but both are natural, just as natural as health and disease.

Spontaneous organization, moreover, has cumulative effects. Let us imagine a nation the citizens of which gather spontaneously into associations polarized towards the national good. Obviously there is a natural co-ordination of efforts amongst all the institutions thus created, whether they be official or public. A kind of convergence will gradually result from the fact that they all tend towards the common weal, and therefore the efficiency of the whole, in the economic and scientific sense of the term, will reach its maximum. While,

The Natural Structure

if the spirit of spontaneous organization is lacking, the few associations which do get started will in all likelihood tend to uphold class or personal interests; thus moved by diverging and incoherent forces, they will be bound to come into conflict with each other, and all of them with the State, and a disastrous waste of energies will fritter away the vitality of the nation.

In the last resort, then, the spirit of spontaneous organization is but a manifestation of the nation's health; i.e. of the fact that the nation's energy flows through its body from the individuals through the several groups towards the whole national being, always in a positive and creative direction. We are thus naturally led to adopt an objective conception of health in a community. Health is the state of a community in which energies always flow in a positive and creative way; i.e. in such a way that every constituent unit receives its energy from a smaller or simpler one and hands on its own energy in a higher form to a more complex unit above it, so that by converging channels the energy is gathered in its highest form into the whole nation.

It will be noticed that this objective conception of health provides us with an equally clear and objective conception of peace, for, as we have just observed, the moment the spirit of spontaneous organization is lacking in a community, the groups or units that arise in its midst are bound to come into conflict. In fact, peace and health in collectivities are words which mean exactly the same thing.

Since we started from the idea that the community

is alive, we assume it has energy. Since it has energy, this energy must perforce manifest itself either in conflict (war) or in harmony (peace). There is one only way of ensuring the flow of energy in peace: to canalize it along one single direction along the tree of life. This can be done in two senses: from the parts to the whole, or from the whole to the parts. The first means life always integrated into higher and higher forms; the second means life always disintegrated into lower and lower forms. The first is organization, the second is corruption. Corruption is no doubt a form of life. It may be defined as the state in which the parts live at the expense of the whole until its ultimate destruction. Corruption is therefore the backwash, the ebbing out of a wave of life. From the point of view of the universe, it is as much life as organization; but from the point of view of the particular "whole" which is being disintegrated, it is stark death. It follows that peace, in the creative and living sense of the word, demands that the flow of energy run along the integrating direction, i.e. from the parts to the whole.

Let us now consider for a moment any one of the units within the nation. It will have below it a series of sets of units or groups, simpler and simpler, until we come to the single individual; above it another series of groups, more and more complicated, until we come to the nation. That being so, it is obviously impossible to ensure the health of the nation below the point which is under observation without ensuring it above this point. For if the flow of energy

The Natural Structure

comes from the simpler to the more complex units up to a certain point, it cannot be reversed just at this point without destroying the health and peace of the whole system. Therefore no unit lesser than the nation can deflect to its own selfish use the energies which it receives from below without impairing the health of the whole nation, and therefore its own health. In fact, any attempt at deflecting the collective energies in their healthy flow from the parts to the whole, to the benefit of the unit placed in the stream of life, is sheer corruption, and as such carries within it the germ of death.

We are now in a position to extend our ideas of peace and health to the world community. It is obvious that we cannot manufacture peace, nor negotiate it, nor muddle through to it, nor build it up by dint of patient and ingenious labour. For peace is one of the forms of health of the community; and the health of the community is not a matter of volition but a matter of fact. The world community will not attain peace until its energies flow undisturbed in the collective and positive direction, from the parts to the whole, without any "corrupt" deflection in favour of a blindly selfish lesser unit. Now we all know that nations are all blind in this respect. The best of them endeavour to secure health and peace within their internal territory; (surely a material and puerile conception of what a nation is, a mistake similar to that which human beings make in identifying themselves with, and limiting their personalities to, the body). But even the best of nations consider it as their higher duty to deflect such energy as they can to their immediate benefit instead of letting it flow in the direction of life and health towards the world community; i.e. even the best of nations, considered as units of the world community, are corrupt.

The way to peace is therefore clear. We must ensure that the energies of the world flow freely in the healthy direction, from the parts to the whole. In so far as this aim is sought within the limits of national life, it means that world peace depends on the development of national patriotism, i.e. of the healthy subordination of all the units lesser than the nation to the national whole; in so far as this aim is sought outside the boundaries of national life, it means we must seek to awake in men a world patriotism which will integrate nations as units within the wider whole.

It will be noticed that, when thus strictly defined and rightly understood, world peace, far from being inconsistent with national patriotism and opposed to it, is strictly dependent and inseparable from a patriotic spirit, both in theory and in practice.

10. THE CRISIS

The perfectly healthy man does not exist. Rather than an actual human being he is an idea, an abstraction which enables us to gravitate towards health as best we can. The perfectly healthy nation exists no more than the perfectly healthy man. It is but an idea which may be useful as a guide towards the understanding of collective life. Just as geometric

The Natural Structure

figures, in spite of the fact that they cannot be materialized, are indispensable not only for all space-thinking but even for all activities which develop in space and deal with matter such as architecture, town-planning, railway building, so this conception of health, a pure abstraction, is nevertheless one of the most important and potent sources of right activity in the world of men.

Though his usual condition be more or less distant from the inaccessible state of perfect health, man refuses to consider it as his normal state. A normal state is that which fits in with the norm, even though the norm, being a perfect idea, is in itself impossible to realize in actual fact. Yet, owing to the existence of this concept of the norm, a tension arises in our will between the usual state in which we live and the normal state at which we aim. This tension is a powerful spring for betterment and progress.

As with individuals, so with nations. Lack of health, however, in men as well as in nations may be due to organic or to functional causes, i.e. to an incapacity for achieving the essential balance of the energies, which is health—an incapacity which may be inherent, or merely due to insufficient growth; or to a temporary disturbance of such a balance of energies which impairs the right working of the organism, and may end in permanently injuring it; or, finally, it may be due to a defective adaptation to environment.

Now the crisis the world is undergoing is no doubt due to all these causes at a time. There are some countries in which, for well-known historical reasons, the *people* is defective. Such is the case in practically the whole American continent. In such countries time and an adequate statesmanship may cure this possibly temporary incapacity for developing an adequate relationship between the three layers of the community; but meantime the healthy flow of energy is not attained, and internal strife is the inevitable result. There are again countries which, for reasons inherent in their national psychology, find it extremely hard to evolve the upper layers of their national constitution. This is in particular the case in ultra-individualistic nations, such as the three Mediterranean peninsulas, and most particularly Spain. Here the individual is so strong a centre of polarization that energies are apt to flow at least as much towards him as towards the nation; *corruption* (in our sense of the word) is rampant; the rising of the bourgeoisie above the people and of the aristocracy above the bourgeoisie occurs, but with the utmost difficulty and in an antagonistic and fiercely equalitarian field of forces; and thus the health of the community is never reached, and internal peace becomes an utter impossibility.

There are again countries in which, also for reasons of national psychology, the rise of the bourgeoisie is fairly easy, but not so that of the aristocracy. Such is the case, though in different ways, in France and in the United States of America. In France the individualistic tendency of the nation finds an easy outlet in the creation of an expert and highly cultivated middle class; one of the finest

The Natural Structure

examples of bourgeoisie the world has ever known. But the equalitarian sense of the race on the one hand, and an excessive intellectualism on the other hand, hinder the rise of an aristocracy of statesmen. This explains why the French are more successful in political and social tactics than in political and social strategy. They do things well even though the things they do are not the best that could be done in the circumstances. They win all the rounds, and lose the match. In foreign affairs their diplomacy is good and their policy poor.

In the United States of America, where the people, as we have had occasion to note, is the weak feature in the social structure, there is but little aristocracy. It might then be said that the United States of America is but a huge bourgeoisie, if it were possible for a nation to possess a bourgeoisie at all without a people and an aristocracy; these conceptions being essentially organic, and therefore mutually dependent. In saying that the United States of America has but little aristocracy, we do not refer to the fact that America, having no historical tradition from bygone monarchical days, has no blue blood in her higher social levels. By aristocracy we mean, as has more than once been pointed out in these pages, a class of statesmen and patricians devoted to the public good and capable of conceiving it in its vastness and complexity. The reasons for this weakness of the aristocratic element in the United States of America are not far to seek. Let us first point out in passing that there are two types of aristocracy in our Western societies, related respectively by ties and subtle affinity with the people and with the bourgeoisie. There is first the aristocracy with the stress on action, on immediate experience, and on the professions and occupations which go with it, such as hunting, farming, exploration, and war; the model for this aristocracy is still to be found in England. And then there is the intellectual type of aristocracy, which rises above mere knowledge and training but nevertheless out of them. The model of this aristocracy is to be found in Switzerland.

Now in the United States the people is too weak a social element to produce the English type of the middle class, and too indifferent to disinterested knowledge and training to produce the Swiss type. The United States are therefore the victims of an excessive utilitarian conception of education. Of the two duties of the bourgeoisie, their middle class is trained only for the first: expert knowledge and craftsmanship; it is definitely backward with regard to the second: general culture and an outlook on life. Now it is precisely from this second zone of middle-class development that the intellectual variety of the aristocracy of States is expected to rise.

It follows that, though aristocratic qualities are available—and generously so—they are turned away from the service of the nation towards that of lesser interests. The best brains of the Republic are in "business," while in England, or in Switzerland, they are in public affairs—politics or the civil service. Curiously enough, the American business man is often of a distinctly aristocratic type, and while

The Natural Structure

remaining in business, with all that business implies in hardness and competitive keenness, he often has a public-spirited, liberal, and even generous view of his profession. It seems as if a very little more would suffice to make of him an aristocrat in the English way, i.e. a statesman. But this little more is not forthcoming. It may be that the unpleasant features of the vote-catching machinery of politics keep him off, in a Coriolanus sort of mood. But though this may be one of the reasons for his reserve, there is no doubt that the main cause must be found in the absence of a robust popular basis for the American nation, for it is only on the basis of a people—an organic, human groundwork—that the community can evolve an aristocracy conscious of its public duties. Otherwise the State appears merely as yet another business, and the business man prefers his own, thus depriving his nation and the world of genuine gifts of statesmanship.

The two societies which come nearest to our conception of a healthy nation are England and Switzerland. There are others, such as the Scandinavian States and Holland. But England and Switzerland have the advantage of standing out as two clearly defined types of healthy nation, while the others would partake in different proportions of the English and the Swiss aspects. England and Switzerland are both rich in spontaneous organization, as a kind of gift in their citizens, who for this reason rightly give the impression of being *goodnatured*. England owes her splendid sense of continuity to the peaceful development of the empirical turn of her people. A set of historical circumstances acting in co-operation with her national character have determined the peculiar, liberal rather than democratic, flavour of her commonwealth. Her aristocrat is used to command and to expect obedience, for he takes for granted that he was born for it. Hence a certain continuity in her aristocracy, which thus becomes a class, not merely in the *natural*, but in the current *social* sense of the word. There is a close contact between the aristocracy and the people; a closer one perhaps than between the middle class and either of the other two classes. And thus the aristocrat realizes from his earliest days that he has a mission to fulfil, and that he can only justify his privileges by serving the people. In Switzerland the circumstances of history and the national character have set the stress on democracy rather than liberty. The aristocracy is but an offshoot of the bourgeoisie —a bourgeoisie, moreover, which is as well trained in special knowledge as the American and as widely educated in general ideas as the French. There are no great ranges of personal fortune in the nation, so that the distances between the three classes are never very great.

But even the best-organized communities, the "healthiest" ones, suffer from temporary troubles and from changes in environment. There is a constant source of ill health in countries—the corruptive effect of power. Aristocracies, even in the best nations, evince a greater or lesser tendency to the selfish exploitation of their privileges, and particularly of their privilege of governing. In the social sphere this evil has given rise to socialism. No one can read the industrial history of the nineteenth century without realizing that the abject oblivion of their duties on the part of those who should have been the aristocrats of industry has been the true cause of the movement now breaking like a gigantic wave over the whole world. The error in this huge socialistic movement is that it seeks to destroy the very institution of aristocracy—an utter impossibilty; while what it ought to seek is its purification. But it cannot be doubted that the aristocracy which has so far governed the world has in the majority of cases, though not in all, deserved its fate.

Another and a very potent cause of social disturbance is the growth of a disproportionate working population in most modern communities. This phenomenon is typical of England. England might have developed into one of the happiest communities in the world had she remained predominantly agricultural, for the balance between her countryside people, her university-educated middle classes, and her squirearchy and aristocracy would have become nearly perfect in the nineteenth century. We should then have witnessed a country governed with wisdom and self-denial by an aristocracy along liberal-democratic lines, really and genuinely in the interests of the people. But the industrial revolution in the beginning of the nineteenth century came unfortunately to infect this beautiful land with the black pox of industry, and soon the huge working class and a large proletariat came to complicate her social scheme and to afflict her mind with the worries of unemployment, the shame of slums, and the ugliness of misery. Thus the relations between her three natural classes were deeply disturbed, and the way was paved for the introduction in her midst of the baneful doctrine of class war.

Finally, a profound change in environment has come to impair further still the health of all modern nations. The contemporary world is so complex that government has become a highly technical craft. The subject has been dealt with in other sections of this book, and needs no new development here. It is merely recalled in order to show that the growing technical complication of collective life amounts to a change of environment for the community and demands a change in the type of aristocracy that is wanted. Leadership must gradually evolve from the English to the Swiss type; from the traditional aristocratic liberal and empirical type to the scientific bourgeois, democratic, and expert type. Now these adjustments are not easy, since they imply questions of personal destiny and education, growth and adaptation. Some grinding of the springs is to be expected at the turn of the way.

Nor should we, when dealing with changes of environment, leave aside the profound effects which some modern inventions must be having on our collective psychology. The very basis of this psychology—the subconscious wealth of the people—is being sapped by such powerful eye-openers as the cinema and the radio set. Through eyes and ears the community, not merely the national but the world community, is daily pouring impressions and emo-

The Natural Structure

tions, possibly not the best ones, on the countryside, once a haven of peace isolated from urban turmoils. The indifference with which this grave fact, pregnant with unpredictable consequences, is watched—or perhaps overlooked—by a supercilious aristocracy is baffling to the mind. A continuous flow of concrete images of action—instant, telling, sensational, brutal even—which the cinema pours on the people, i.e. on the subconscious part of the nation, is bound to cause a psychical revolution of almost unfathomable depths. The consequences can be observed already on the people itself and on the two other layers of the community. And we are perhaps only at the mere beginning of this far-reaching change.

And finally there is another change of environment, which is deeply disturbing to the health of even the sanest nations. A world community is being born under our eyes. It is a new community. It has its people—the whole of mankind; but it is just beginning to evolve its bourgeoisie—the enlightened world citizens who try to master the technique of world events; and it has not yet been able to create its aristocracy: there are no world statesmen.

Most of the searching evils of our time come from this disastrous void. The fact that the World War let loose on mankind problems of world size, which found no men of world size to deal with them, is responsible for the dislocation of world affairs both material and mental which is leading everywhere to paralysis of trade, unemployment, civil war, revolution, and possibly another world war.

The rise of the world community is in itself a

change of environment which requires new gifts for our bourgeoisie, and above all for our aristocracy. The blind and wrathful movement which seeks the destruction of those two institutions is but the irrational expression of this idea. It is useless to expect peace until a world aristocracy is evolved. But we know that a community can only evolve its aristocracy when it enjoys health. We are then, as ever with life, in a vicious circle; but, as ever with life, we can escape from it by courage and the determination to create new conditions and a new world.

The health of the world community requires the growth of world patriotism; it demands that nations should purify their corrupt nationalism, and sincerely pour their energies into the wider organism which is awaiting their intelligent sacrifices to grow and become strong. Not till world patriotism rises triumphant over national patriotism can we expect health and peace for the world community, for our own nations, for our families, and for ourselves.

CHAPTER V

Methods of the Unanimous Organic Democracy

RECAPITULATION OF PRINCIPLES

OUR study of present-day collective life has led us to adopt a certain number of constructive ideas which may serve as a basis for the constitution of a modern State. These ideas are:

1. That the finality of life is in man and not in the State.
2. That man's aim in life—individual experience—implies the greatest individual liberty possible.
3. That freedom of thought is as indispensable for the individual as for the State.
4. That inequality is natural and good, both for the individual and for the community.
5. That in functions the individual serves the State, while in values the State serves the individual.
6. That the functional State, i.e. the economic and financial State, must be organized as an efficient piece of machinery; but that, upon it, there must rise the moral and political State based on liberal and democratic principles.
7. That private initiative in economic matters is indispensable to liberty.
8. That the State has the right and the duty to set limits to both liberty and inequality, so that the more ambitious citizens do not become too powerful nor the more slothful too indigent.

Unanimous Organic Democracy

9. That citizenship should be limited to active citizens carefully selected, and that the government should be an "aristocracy."
10. That the State has sovereignty as a matter of common sense.
11. That this sovereignty is limited in all that concerns war, and that the State has no right to require military service in wars contrary to the international law prevailing.
12. That the natural and necessary form of the State is that of a unanimous organic democracy, towards which all contemporary democracy must tend if our civilization is to be saved.

While these general ideas apply to all liberal democracies, the ways of applying them are of course to be studied in relation to the psychology of the people concerned. Many of the disappointments which liberal democracy has had to undergo in more than one country have been due to a disregard for the effects of climate and race on political principles. The greatest of these disappointments is the obvious discredit which has afflicted the parliamentary system in practically every country outside of Great Britain. Parliament in England owes its success to two conditions: the first is the existence of a very small number of political parties, usually two; this in turn is but the political manifestation of the spirit of sport, which is only fully satisfied when there are two teams, each under the orders of a captain: the second is the peculiar dislike of the Englishman for ideas in themselves, and his craving for results in terms of action. These two conditions are essential to the success of the parliamentary system, and they are present in England to an extraordinary degree. But the majority of the nations which have somewhat bookishly imitated English parliamentary institutions have found, to their sorrow, that the English system cannot be transplanted into the psychological soil of other nations.

The following pages are therefore written bearing in mind these sobering thoughts on the relativity of political forms and their dependence on time and place.

THE ECONOMIC STATE

The structure of the State must reflect the clear separation implied in the principles mentioned above. (Nos. 5 and 6.)

Since in functions the individual serves the State while in values the State serves the individual, it is natural that the functional State should adopt a more rigid structure than the politico-moral State, to which pertains a greater liberalism.

The modern State should separate as clearly as possible its political and its economic functions. It is true that, in actual life, the line may be somewhat blurred; but the means for handling doubtful cases could easily be devised empirically. The division might be attempted in the following way:

To the political State would correspond:

(1) All *final* decisions involving sovereignty, including decisions on economic questions.

Unanimous Organic Democracy

(2) Constitutional affairs.
(3) Foreign relations.
(4) National defence.
(5) Home affairs, justice, and police.
(6) Education (technical education a doubtful case).
(7) Information (Press, radio, cinematograph).

To the economic State would correspond:

(1) The study and organization of the national economy.
(2) General direction of production and distribution and the study of consumption.
(3) Public works.
(4) Finance, Treasury, and credit control (with the Budget as a frontier case).
(5) Industrial (Guild) organization.
(6) Management of communications, including the Merchant Service and commercial aviation.

The organization of the Economic State should be based on efficiency. It would have to put the stress on authority, hierarchy, and discipline. At the head of this State there should be an Economic Council selected for its competence, and by no manner of means to act as a clearing-house for conflicting interests. It should be the thinking brain and organizer of the national interest. This body should be the only initiator of economic and financial legislation and should, besides, have executive power in the management of credit-note circulation, and in general of all that influences prices directly and is or ought to be the privilege of the State.

The Economic Council should create and direct

The Methods

a centre of economic and financial information both national and international. This centre should be at the disposal of the producers and distributors of the wealth of the country; on the basis of this information the Economic Council would *lead* the national economy. This leadership might vary from a firm handling, amounting almost to dictatorship, which would centralize the whole national economy under the direction of the National Council, to a mild, discretional, and advisory function guiding producers and consumers and, in general, the national economy along more or less definitely set lines of development. All would depend on the country and the time: thus a primitive country from the economic point of view would have to be more firmly led than a highly developed community; and times of intense emergency or of economic crisis would in any one country lead the Economic Council to tighten the screw of its centralization.

The Economic Council should be the apex of the organization of the Economic State. It is as well to note that this State will have to fulfil the following conditions:

(1) To respect a considerable nucleus of private initiative.
(2) To prevent the accumulation of excessive power in the hands of any one citizen or group of citizens.
(3) To prevent the exploitation of labour.
(4) To create a sufficient variety of occupation to absorb the wayward and ambitious as well as those who are not ambitious and prefer stability.

(5) To prevent the disorganization of the public services by industrial strife and the abuse of the strike for political ends.
(6) To allow the play of necessity, but to stop it short of destitution.

This programme of requirements cannot be met by means of a simple panacea. Such things are only to be found in books, pamphlets, and propaganda papers. The solution must be sought in groups of convergent measures, preferably indirect and automatic, and continuously watched over by intelligent and disinterested people, that is to say by the Economic Council.

The framework of the Economic State would be constituted by a certain number of public institutions (*institutions de droit public*) entrusted with the following services:

(1) Fuel. (The mining and transforming of coal; petroleum and mineral oils; industrial alcohol.)
(2) Power, light, and water.
(3) Iron and steel.
(4) Communications by land, air, and sea.
(5) Banking.
(6) Cereals and their transformations.
(7) Any other big industry the development of which would make it a predominant element in the country.

These public institutions might undergo a greater or lesser degree of socialization according to the different countries. In some nations the best form would be that of a State industry, such as are the

The Methods

post and telegraphs in almost all countries. Thus England, Germany, and the Scandinavian countries need not hesitate to adopt this course, since experience of their State services shows that the bureaucracy in these countries is capable of exercising industrial functions. But countries where existing State services do not justify this confidence would have to be content with a hybrid form. A company, capitalistic in its form, might be constituted in which the State would have a predominant voice as to capital, profits, and management. The State here, be it remembered, would not be the political, but the economic State, represented by the National Economic Council.

Whatever their degree of socialization, these public institutions would possess the following characteristics:

(1) Ownership of the source of wealth vested in the nation, except in complicated cases like banking and cereals, which would require more detailed consideration.

(2) Capital guaranteed and supervised by the State; dividends limited by law.

(3) Labour guaranteed employment; rate of real wage; right to old age pensions; wage during illness; paid holidays; in fine, all the advantages of permanent officials.

(4) In the case therefore of both capital and labour, minimum of private initiative, maximum of security.

(5) The lock-out and strike, illegal; associations of either employers or workers aiming at industrial strife, illegal.

Unanimous Organic Democracy

Within each of these industries or groups of industries a Guild organization would be adopted. Each group would unite its men under three orders: manual workers, administrative workers, technical workers. From these three orders a Council would be elected. The national organization, framed in parallel fashion, would culminate in a Guild Council. The powers of this Council would differ according to the degree of socialization achieved by the said public institution. To take two extreme cases:

A semi-capitalistic, semi-State-owned enterprise (the minimum of socialization here considered) would be administered by a bicameral system: the Governing Body and the Guild Council. Both would have executive powers of internal administration subject to a general statute for the industry concerned, approved by the Economic State. The Guild Council would specialize more particularly on questions of personal discipline and the technical organization of work, while the Governing Body would specialize in general policy. Neither would have executive, but only advisory, powers in matters beyond the boundary of the Guild, and therefore concerning the general economy of the nation. For instance, if we suppose the railway system of the country to be constituted by a public institution of a semi-State type, it would be administered by a Governing Body composed of representatives of capital who would necessarily include a majority of representatives of the State chosen by the Economic Council, removed from all political influence, and by a Guild Council comprising equal numbers of

The Methods

technical, administrative, and manual workers. Questions of personal discipline and internal policy would be solved by common agreement between the two organs. But everything that concerned tariffs, construction of new lines, and, in general, all matters affecting the general economy, could only be examined by them as advisory bodies and would have to be referred to higher authorities for decision.

The other extreme case is that in which the public institutions are totally socialized. In this case the Governing Body is entirely composed of State representatives, but their respective relations and powers would be identical with those mentioned above.

Within the framework of these public institutions private initiative, both on the side of capital and on that of labour, would have free scope in general industry. This would be the field of those who prefer liberty to security. Fate here would have a wider range for good or for bad, and whoever ventured on this ground would have no right to claim the help of the State in his failures, since the State would not ask a share in his successes. Following on the principle of minimum and maximum limits to avoid, on the one hand, destitution, and on the other excessive power, a minimum real wage and a maximum dividend would have to be established; but the margin in both cases would be larger than in the public industries. As a State or semi-State organism is not always the best ground for the selection of leaders, the field of private enterprise might act as a stimulus to the public services and as a training-ground for the leaders of big industry.

These industries, for all that they would remain under private enterprise, would nevertheless be grouped into guilds for purposes of internal organization and for the collective study of their respective problems. Although a looser organization than that of the public industries, the guilds of private enterprises would centralize and distribute technical information, smooth the relations between capital and labour, and constitute electoral bodies from which would issue the Guild Congress.

The Guild Congress would be composed of representatives of all the Guilds. It would be convened by the Economic Council whenever necessary. It would act:

(1) As the clearing house of the Guilds in order to co-ordinate their work and organization.
(2) As the legislative house on economic and financial questions.
(3) As an advisory organ of the National Economic Council.

This organization would seek to realize the aims set out above by a policy of watchful activity, applying in particular the following methods:

(1) Control of the Banks, especially as to the creation and distribution of credit.
(2) Issue and withdrawal of money.
(3) Control of the big industries, above all those not organized as public institutions, with a view to avoiding the creation of groups powerful enough to upset the balance of the State.
(4) Limitation of large landed property.

The Methods

(5) Limitation of private fortunes.
(6) The organization of a system to avoid strikes and lock-outs in the industries in which they are not forbidden by law. The main object of the Guild is to make them useless as economic weapons. As political weapons they cannot be justified.

The matter of unemployment deserves special consideration. The modern Economic State cannot adopt any of the points of view at present prevailing. We are, as always in life, held by pairs of opposites. If we leave things to themselves, we make straight for poverty and demoralization; if we intervene too much, we have the "Stable"-State, where citizens are like well-groomed horses rather than men on their own mettle. The dole is a premium on idleness; to refuse it is to punish the unemployed worker. On the whole the arguments against the dole are overwhelming on both economic and moral grounds. But the moral duty of the State to do all in its power to find work—as distinct from "the right of the worker to work," which is an empty phrase—is undeniable. The ethical and economic aspects of this difficult question would be considerably simplified if, when the institutions of public law are created, a large number of workers become State officials, for whom unemployment is unknown. For the others private enterprise, in its higher salaries, would offer no small compensation for the risk of unemployment. The State, besides, might help in two ways:

By creating a *voluntary fund of insurance* against unemployment, to which the worker, in times of high wages, would contribute in order to insure himself against his own unemployment.

By establishing lists of *marginal public works*, which the State would undertake only at times of crisis when the lowering of the interest on capital and the index of wages would make their construction at that level of cost pay.

THE POLITICAL STATE

Above the Economic State, based on order, information, efficiency, and authority, there rises the Political State. While the Economic State organizes the individuals to serve it, the Political State is the servant of the men who compose the nation. This, then, is the sphere of democracy and of the sovereignty of the people.

But by democracy we mean organic democracy, and by sovereignty of the people we mean the competent and considered opinion of the nation ascertained in the most authoritative manner.

At the basis of the Political State we must place the notion of *active citizenship*. This notion implies that mere existence does not suffice to acquire citizenship, nor even paying taxes, which after all are recuperated in services. Citizenship must be won in two ways: negatively, by the omission of acts against the State; positively, by activities of benefit to the community. It is more difficult to define in detail the positive than the negative conditions, and only by way of example we indicate the following:

Contributions to the upkeep of beneficent, educa-

The Methods

tional, or political associations, with due inspection to prevent the system from degenerating into the creation of artificial citizens at the disposal of the wealthy; taking part in properly controlled groups for the study of public problems; public or social services duly recognized; competence objectively demonstrated, etc. The most difficult point in carrying out this discrimination would be how to set up the authorities beyond all suspicion of partiality who would decide the granting of citizenship. But this principle is of such great importance that, in spite of the difficulties it presents in practice, it will be necessary to apply it if the political level of the democracies of the future is to be raised.

The citizens would form the basis of the municipal electorate. They would thus be called to pronounce upon issues directly concerning themselves and upon persons with whose activities they were familiar. But their right of direct suffrage would go no further than the municipality. No apology is offered for thus discarding the time-honoured principle of direct suffrage, because direct suffrage has been honoured more by time than by use. One of the causes of its failure is, curiously enough, that it does not exist. For under the system prevailing in all democracies, with trifling exceptions, the so-called elections by direct suffrage are always elections of the second degree. The first stage consists of the *secret* election of candidates by the parties; the second, of the public election of members by the electors. The electors do not elect whom they want, but whom they can: and their election has to be limited to the small margin of choice which the list of candidates offers. On the other hand, the first stage of this election is carried out by partial and irresponsible people. We all know to what discredit this system has led Parliaments. Instead of these spurious and insincere practices, the modern State should limit the elector's function to the area of his direct observation, i.e. to the municipal field.

The municipal councillors would form the electorate for the county or regional legislature. Following the same principle, the regional legislators would form the electorate to elect the Political Assembly. The Political Assembly would elect the Government.

The objection will certainly be raised that municipal assemblies are usually the hot-bed of professional politicians and the worst possible basis for the electoral pyramid. This objection is based on the observation of municipal assemblies recruited by present-day methods. But three new circumstances must be borne in mind: the first is that we are assuming an electoral body purified by the measures put into practice in electing citizens; the second that the municipality will act as a centre of attraction for very different people once it itself constitutes part of the electoral body on a wider territory; the third, that financial and economic questions will not be resolved by it, but will be relegated to the Economic State. In these conditions a change for the better in the staffing and ways of municipalities might well be expected without undue optimism.

The functions of the Political Assembly would differ according to whether the matters dealt with

The Methods

were political or economic. In political matters—including constitutional affairs—the Political Assembly would work like the Swiss Parliament or the American Congress. In particular, the Political Assembly would discuss and vote the Budget, though the Budget, no doubt, should be carefully studied at first by the Economic Council and by the Guild Assembly. In economic matters the procedure would be different; we have seen that the initiative in legislation belongs to the Economic Council. The Guild Assembly would discuss the propositions giving them form of law. The Political Assembly would vote them in exercise of its sovereign functions, or would send them back for further study by the Technical Assembly, or would refuse its vote absolutely if its opposition were one of principle. A mixed commission of the two Houses, which could be easily organized, could deal with doubtful cases. The Political Assembly would be competent to alter the constitution of the Economic State, but only after hearing the opinions of the Guild Assembly and the Economic Council.

Stability would be the main preoccupation of the modern State. To this end the following constitutional precautions should be taken:

(1) *The Government to be elected for four years*, the same period as the Political Assembly which would elect it. It is evident that, in practice, whatever constitutional precautions be adopted to secure the stability of a Government which depends on the confidence of a House, the life of a ministry is always at the mercy of Parliament.

Unanimous Organic Democracy

The House could always reverse its vote and withdraw its confidence directly, or indirectly, from the Government of its choice. But the fact that the Government is elected for four years is already of itself a certain guarantee of stability in the same way as a House elected for four years considers this period as its normal life, even though the head of the State has the power to dissolve it. The following guarantees of stability would, however, be added:

(2) *The fall of the Government would imply automatically the dissolution of the House.* This rule is justified both in theory and in practice. In theory, since a House which brings down a government of its choice disavows itself; in practice, since the fall of ministries is generally due to the aspirations of Members of Parliament with ministerial ambitions. By substituting the certainty of new elections for the probability of political promotion the stability of the Government would increase, for it would reverse the direction in which the motives of Members act. On the other hand, there is not so much apprehension of frequent dissolutions of Parliament in a system under which new elections would mobilize a much smaller electoral body than is the case with universal suffrage.

(3) *The Budget would be voted for two years.* This rule also is justified both in theory and in practice. In theory, because the increasing complexity of economic life necessitates a biennial Budget; in practice, because in this way the House would be deprived of the weapon most frequently employed by Parliaments to abuse their power against the executive. On the other

The Methods

hand, in the system here put forward the Budget would form part of the groups of laws which, owing to their technical character, would be initiated and prepared by the Economic Council and the Guild Assembly. On account, however, of the great political importance of the Budget, both in regard to the proper endowing of the purely political Departments of the State and in what appertains to the political character of taxation, it is indispensable that the Budget should also be discussed in the Political Assembly; it is therefore advisable that the modern State should grant the time required so that, first the Economic Council with the Government, then the Guild Assembly, and finally the Political Assembly, can devote the necessary attention to this affair. To that effect the two-yearly period is absolutely indispensable.

One point remains to be settled. How is the National Economic Council to be appointed? It is essential that special precautions should be taken to ensure freedom from all political interference, and that the selection should be made solely on the basis of competence. The details of the election would obviously depend on the special circumstances of each country. As a mere matter of suggestion we might propose that the National Economic Council, composed of a number of councillors varying, say, from nine to twenty-one, should be selected by the coincident vote of the Government and the existing Economic Council from a list of three times as many names as there are candidates, drawn up by the Guild Assembly by a majority of two-thirds. The nomination would be for nine years, but every three years one-third of the members would drop out and either be re-elected or replaced.

No doubt this system would be complex and difficult to work. But so is the present system. For instance, the objection might be raised that the issue of public loans is a matter which no Government can delegate; and yet, under this system, it might be the prerogative of the Economic Council. The answer to this is that no present-day Governments would dare to issue a loan without consulting, and even at times asking the permission of, the occult and irresponsible powers which direct finance. The issue of a loan has three aspects: political, financial, and economic. The last two would fall entirely within the province of the National Economic Council, while the first would be a specific attribute of the Government. But the adjustment of the competencies does not need to be an insuperably difficult task, and if it acted as a break to possible fantasies of the political power, it would be all to the good for the nation. After all, it is difficult to put as an objection the very virtue with which we are endeavouring to endow the State—liberation of the national economy from all political interference and its redemption from the private powers which to-day hold it enslaved.

INTERNATIONAL ASPECTS

In thus organizing the State so that economic matters are under the aegis of efficiency and objec-

The Methods

tivity, we provide incidentally an adequate national solution for adjusting national economies into an international harmonious whole. We know that this problem is to-day essential. Mechanical progress has made the world one single market, and the fever of economic nationalism from which all nations to-day are suffering can appear as the failure of internationalism only to superficial minds, since its very universality is but a confirmation of the world-wide character of present-day economics. *All nations, that is all the cells of the world unit, are afflicted by the same disease.* It is not then a national trouble, but a world-trouble that can only be cured by world-remedies. The present epidemic of economic nationalism is due partly to political, partly to financial causes, and in both cases to the failure of the world to organize itself as a political and economic unit, when in fact it is so; that is to say its failure to become one as a subject, although it is already one as an object. To-day wars are world-wars and international questions are world-questions, but the world has been unable to evolve a world-policy or a world-finance, and the nations entrench themselves, in mutual suspicion, behind their political frontiers and their trade barriers as a sick man might shut himself up in his room, not as a remedy but as a symptom of his disease.

Now, limiting for the moment our argument to the financial and economic side, it is obvious that the remedy lies in a federation of national economies. Therefore the time has come when, even if the step were not advisable on national grounds, international reasons would recommend a centralization of national economies. Every nation should, therefore, organize its economic life so that, without sacrificing any of the essential liberties, there is a head to think and act, and therefore to negotiate. When the economic life of every nation is made independent of politics, yet remains vigorously organized under the national sovereignty, the co-ordination of all the national economies into a harmonious whole will be much less difficult than it is to-day.

Moreover, it seems natural to hope that the evolution of world economics will tend towards a federation of great public services such as those outlined above under the name of Institutions of Public Law. For our part, for exclusively international reasons, based on what is called *Disarmament* but is in reality the *organization of Peace*, we have been advocating since 1928 the organization of Civil Aviation as a world institution of public law under the authority of the League of Nations. For reasons of the same order, though less urgent, it might be advisable to study the possibility of organizing in a similar way the fuel industries, the Mercantile Marine, the production of iron and steel, the distribution of cereals, and perhaps some other industries. Such an evolution would be admirably prepared if within the national framework the institutions of public law, which, in our opinion, must constitute the main lines of the Economic State, had already been in operation. In this way the Economic State we have sketched justifies itself, not merely on national grounds, but also from the

The Methods

point of view of the organization of the world economy, that is to say of peace.

THE PRESS

It is easier to criticize the private ownership of the Press than to find remedies for the situation it creates in a modern State. Private ownership of the Press has given the world a few excellent organs of opinion and a fairly large number of good newspapers; but in exchange it has allowed a scandalous exploitation of the foibles of human nature and, by the power thus obtained, a systematic distortion of facts and opinions. In any case it is inadmissible, on principle, that an institution of so much political power should be in private hands.

The first solution which occurs to the mind is to include the Press in the list of public institutions proposed when outlining the Economic State. But the very fact that in so doing we should be relegating to the Economic State an activity so essentially political as the Press, and assimilating information and dialectics to coal, iron, or water, points to this being the wrong road. Before choosing another it might be as well to distinguish and separate the three different aspects under which we may consider the Press:

(1) The Press as an industry.
(2) The Press as an agency for distributing news.
(3) The Press as a forum.

For an adequate solution of the problem of the Press

it is necessary to take into account the different nature of these three forms of activity.

The Press as an industry could certainly be organized as an institution of public law. Given the enormous importance of its economy and publicity and the primary obligation of the modern State to guard against the undue influence, through this channel, of economics on politics, it would seem almost indispensable to organize the Press as an industry in such a way that all the newspapers of the country, considered as manufactured articles, should be produced under the same economy, and therefore by one single enterprise entrusted with their manufacture. This enterprise would make the contracts for publicity, the profits of which would offset the cost of the unit of production in an absolutely impartial manner as regards the political colour of each paper. The enterprise would of course be a public institution which, owing to its total lack of political influence, could be organized in exactly the same way as the other enterprises which were considered when outlining the Economic State.

The Press, as an agency for the supply of information, has lost some of its importance since the discovery of other mechanical methods of quick communication, such as the radio and the cinematograph; still, what remains is incalculable. Precisely for this reason it would be contrary to the real interests of the community to put the Press under the direct control of the State, for we know that accurate information is an indispensable condition of political freedom. Nevertheless, it is equally im-

The Methods

possible to allow the present system to continue. For though the information which reaches the public may not always be distorted by Government influence, it is frequently deformed by the influence of private interests on the owners of the Press as a commercial enterprise. On the other hand, the requirements of international propaganda, in which all nations in the present state of politics have to indulge, have led fatally to the setting up and developing of news agencies which are only able to exist at all thanks to the consumption of their news by their respective national Presses. As these agencies are aware that their success and prosperity depend, to put it at its lowest, on the goodwill of their Governments and, not infrequently, on generous official subsidies, their liberty of appreciation and their objectivity are very problematical. Such a situation is anything but satisfactory. But what way out is there? Let us observe, at any rate, that it is not to be found by making of information a State service.

The third function which we have attributed to the Press is that of a modern Forum, in which opinions meet and confront each other and views and various political tendencies take shape and find expression. And this brings us to a very similar difficulty. For if private initiative has shown itself powerless in most cases to ensure the impartiality and independence which such a function requires, the organization of the Press as a State institution would prove a worse remedy than the disease, since it would mean the death of all public criticism.

Unanimous Organic Democracy

It seems more than likely that there is no really satisfactory solution of this delicate problem. What we propose here may perhaps be the least bad. As we indicated above, the Press, as an industry for the production of the material object called a newspaper, would be organized as an institution of public law after the model of the others which were to form the Economic State. A news agency would be created with capital from the State granted once and for all, so that the agency could be independent of the Budget. This agency would be managed by a group of men chosen by common agreement from amongst all the political parties for their impartiality and independence of judgment. Such a group or governing board would be answerable to a Court of Arbitration, the constitution of which would vary with each country. The agency would be organized on a guild basis, so that the profession of newsman would be a closed and technical profession. To-day it is an open profession, which is an evil and an unnecessary one. The newsmen of our modern democracies should be specialists, well trained, it goes without saying, in speed and activity, but also as regards good judgment, responsibility, and a sense of proportion, qualities which the commercialized Press of to-day, with few exceptions, neglects deplorably. It is essential for a democracy that the men who keep it informed, who are, so to speak, the nerve terminals of the senses of the community, should be men of good general education, and moreover highly specialized as regards their occupation. The profession of newsman should be one of the noblest and most reputable, as also one of the best paid; but it should also be one of the most exacting in the community. Organized in this way, the agency should put its information free of charge at the disposal of all the newspapers of the country. It would be considered as a public service.

Before touching on the third heading of the solution we are outlining, it would be as well to point out that it is not possible to apply to the Press as Forum, that is to say to the newspaper itself, the same Guild System which was advocated for the Press as Industry and for the Press as Information Agency, because newspapers are not printed solely for news. A certain part of each newspaper has to be edited precisely by newsmen and, in all probability, the agency of information would, in practice, detach a certain number of its newsmen to work in the editorial room of each newspaper. But the news which comes in and is printed as such reappears again more or less transformed and commented on in the editorial paragraph, the special article, and the leading article, and it is quite impossible to draw a line between the commentary on a telegram just received and an article prepared in the editorial room, or the column of collaboration sent by post by some man of letters or science or politics. For this reason the Guild solution is out of the question; but there are other reasons, also, which make it inadvisable for this aspect of the Press. The setting up of a Press Guild, that is to say the handing over of the Press to a guild of newspaper men for them to direct autonomously, would throw an enormous responsibility on the shoulders of one profession. No State could afford to do that. Another solution must be found more consonant with the interests of freedom of thought and of variety of opinion.

The solution might be to place the newspapers of a country at the disposal of political parties or cultural and political associations without lucrative ends. Each party or association would be free to appoint the literary and editorial staff of its own newspapers. The news would be supplied gratis by the agency of information, and the Industrial Guild of the Press would manufacture the newspaper according to a uniform tariff. The accounts of these associations would be public and audited.

To sum up: the future organization of the Press would consist of:

(1) The Industrial Guild of the Press, an institution of public law for the manufacture and sale of newspapers.
(2) The Agency of Information.
(3) The individual newspapers at the disposal of political parties or of special associations.

This is by no means a simple solution, but it might remove the general drawbacks of the present system.

Index

ARISTOCRACY—English aristocracy to-day in contrast with Shakespeare's, 82; basis of good government, 126; defined as natural class, 156, 158, 169; feature of healthy nations, 191; rôle in self-government, 194; two types of aristocracy, 204; evolution needed from English to Swiss type, 208

ARISTOTLE, 148

ARMAMENT FIRMS, 18

ARTISTS, 180

AUTHORITY—relation to liberty, 89, 103; seen as a tendency, 93

BACH, 159

BANKERS—attitude during World War, 18; Professor Soddy on bankers, 62; Federal Reserve Bank and world crisis, 66; choice of governors of central banks, 67; power of bankers, 137

BERNARD SHAW (George) on necessity, 102

BOLSHEVISM (see also *Communism* and *Socialism*)—better than Tsardom, 20; no dictatorship of the people, 20

BOURGEOISIE (see also *Middle Classes*)—defined as natural class, 156, 157, 164; feature of healthy nations, 190; rôle in self-government, 194; rise of bourgeoisie in Russia, 176; pole of gravitation for skilled workers, 175; rôle in culture, 109, 165

BROTHERS KARAMAZOV, the, on liberty, 30

BUJALANCE, 162

BUSINESS MAN (see also *Bankers* and *Finance*)—assumptions, 40; interference in politics, 40; American type, 204

CAPITALISM—theoretical principles, 39; historical rôle, 39; classical exclusion from politics, 40; causes of downfall, 31; inversion of meaning, 41; akin to intellectualism, 51; its theory not science, 130; no longer workable, 151

CHARLES V, 148

CISNEROS (Cardinal Ximenez de), 159

CITIZEN—and inhabitant, 32; behaviour of citizen under an ideal democracy, 37; dispossessed by technique,

237

Index

55; must serve State, 85; citizenship avocation, 124; its restriction advisable, 125; suggestions on citizen for new State, 222

CLASSES—initial unfairness corrected by liberty, 100; classes and inequality, 108; origin, 110; as natural fact, 112, 154; divorce between working and middle classes, 149; Marxist explanation, 145; psychic parallel, 185

CLASS STRUGGLE—and private property, 45; directed against middle class, 46; a fallacy, 110; its explanation, 175

CLEMENCEAU (Georges), 18, 95, 159

COMMUNISM (see also *Bolshevism* and *Socialism*)—issue between Communism and Fascism, 9; enemy of liberty, 10; theory of classless State, 183

CONSCIENTIOUS OBJECTION, 144

COOLIDGE (Calvin)—doctrine on leadership, 53

CORRUPTION—as opposed to organization, 198

CORTÉS (Hernán), 159

CREDIT—its rôle in Society, 61

CRISIS—world crisis analysed, 200

CULTURE—and the State, 79, 85, 104; and bourgeoisie, 109, 165

CUZCO, 163

DARWIN, 148

DEMOCRACY (see *Liberal Democracy*)

DESPOTISM—never a European doctrine, 15

DICTATORSHIPS—world bristling with, 13; in Russia, 13, 20; in Italy, 14, 20; in Germany, 14, 20; as a protest against liberal democracies, 21; inacceptable in principle, 89; liberty of the dictators, 113; dictatorships and plebiscites, 123

DOSTOIEVSKY—on liberty, 30

DREYFUS CASE, 13

ECONOMIC COUNCIL, 214

ECONOMIC STATE, 213

ECONOMIC WEIGHT (see also *Necessity*), 131

ECONOMICS—and the State, 39, 56; and politics, 60, 123; and liberty, 130; the two rival schools of economics, 130

ELECTORATE — competition downwards, 50; suggestions for improvements, 128

ELIZABETH (Queen), 148

EMPLOYERS (see also *Bankers* and *Capitalism*)—tyranny of employers as producers, 57; political power of employers, 57, 60, 119

Index

ENGLAND—attitude during religious wars, 9, 10; standards of liberty, 13; revolution, 14, 15; doctrine of State in old England, 15; historical mission of England, 83; success of Government, 130; education of high classes, 135; a totalitarian State, 148; extremism unknown, 176; self-government, 194; one of two types of aristocracy, 204; nearest type to healthy nation, 205; success of Parliamentary system, 212

EQUALITY (see also *Inequality*)—as understood by classical theorists, 33, 34; and by the masses, 34; and natural privileges, 34; disregard for hierarchy and specialization, 35; and labour, 58; seldom together with liberty, 99, 103

ERASMUS, 14

ESPRIT DES LOIS (see *Montesquieu*)

EUROPE, 7, 8

FASCISM (see also *Dictatorships*)—issue between Fascism and Communism, 9; enemy of liberty, 10; world success of Fascism, 14

FEMINISM—equalitarian prejudice in feminism, 35

FERRER CASE, 13

FINANCE (see also *Bankers* and *Capitalism*) — invasion into politics, 56, 60; power of, 61–64; right of State to limit liberty of, 116; as aristocracy, 181

FRANCE—standards of liberty, 13; revolution, 14, 15; doctrine of State in old, 15; leader of political thought, 15; despotic kings, 28; degeneration of political institutions, 70; historical mission, 83; totalitarian State, 148

FREEDOM OF THOUGHT (see also *Liberty*)—contempt of, in Communism, 9; necessary for politics and for culture, 104; and State, 120

GERMANY, 14, 20

GIOLITTI, 159

GOVERNMENT—by, of, the people, 38; always oligarchy, should be aristocracy, 126

GRANADA, 162

GUILD CONGRESS, 220

HAPPINESS—not man's aim, 85; analysed as equilibrium, 85

HEALTHY NATION (see also *Nation*)—defined, 188; implies bourgeoisie and aristocracy, 190; and spon-

239

Index

taneous organization, 197; world crisis and, 200; nearest types of, 205
HIERARCHY—lesson of war, 19; disregard of, under liberal democracies, 35
HITLER—began as Socialist, 21
HOLLAND, 10, 205
HUARTE — qualifications for kingship, 35

IMPONDERABILIA—in society, 36
INDIVIDUAL—claims all-round freedom, 29; subordination to State, 77; only being with claim to finality, 79; relation to community, 80, 87; his aim experience, 85, 96–98; rights as world citizen, 143
INEQUALITY (see also *Equality*)—basis of collective life, 53; consequence of liberty, 99; comparison with nature, 100; and classes, 108; rôle in selection of leaders, 113; and private initiative, 135
INHABITANT—and citizen, 32
INITIATIVE (see *Private Initiative*)
INTELLECTUALS—disregard for anti-liberal tendencies of communism, 8; gravitation towards capitalism or labour, 50; scarcity of free critics, 52
INTERNATIONAL ECONOMICS, 229

INTERNATIONAL ORGANIZATION, 19
INTERNATIONAL PEACE, 142
INTERNATIONAL SPIRIT, 112
INTERNATIONALIZATION OF POWER, 65
ITALY (see also *Dictatorships*), 14, 20

JEWS, 187

KANT—on individual as an end, 79

LABOUR (see also *Working Classes*) — misconceptions, 43–47; "all wealth comes from labour," 43; private property and labour, 45; exploitation of labour, 57; tyranny of labour as producers, 57; scepticism of labour towards ballot box, 57; and equality, 58; and liberty, 58; and industrial civil war, 119
LEADERSHIP (see also *Aristocracy*)—failure of, 49–53; surrender of leadership by socialist intellectuals, 51; corruption by power, 52; cowardice, 52; weakness towards producers, 59; and freedom of thought, 106; selection of leadership, 128
LEAGUE OF NATIONS, 143, 144, 230

Index

LENIN—herald of dictatorships, 20; his imitators, 21
LEONARDO, 156, 159
LIBERAL DEMOCRACY—Liberal democratic thought between French Revolution and world war, 17; sapped by world war, 17; dislikes socialism, 18; forces against it during war, 19; attacked from left, 20; its weakness as cause of dictatorships, 21; necessity of revision, 22; axioms and postulates of, 25–48; liberal democracy and mass government, 32; disregard of hierarchy, 35; misconceptions over liberal democracy, 36–39; ways and practices, 49–74; statistical conception of liberal democracy, 50, 122; discredited by technique, 54; and by economic and financial forces, 56, 59; dereliction of duty before producers, 59, 119; degeneration of its institutions, 70; open to corruption, 72; organic conception, 19, 77, 122
LIBERTY—threatened by both Fascism and Communism, 8; out of the fashion, 14; as seen by contractual doctrine of State, 16; current misconceptions on it, 27; Montesquieu on it, 27; Rousseau, 28; not primary need of all men, 29, 32; need for revaluation, 33; as seen by labour, 58; relation to authority, 89, 103; relative nature of, 93; as right to misbehave, 95; rôle in State, 97, 104, 120; relation to happiness, 98; to equality, 99, 103; to selection of leaders, 113; its limits, 114, 116; relation to economy, 130; to Marxism, 134; to word citizenship, 143
LLOYD GEORGE, 18
LOUIS XIV, 148

MAISTRE, DE, 186
MAN (see also *Individual*)—above nation, 84, 142; his aim not happiness but experience, 85; psychic constitution of man in parallel with that of society, 184
MARX—and the origin of wealth, 43, 45; a rootless author, 187
MIDDLE CLASSES (see also *Bourgeoisie*, *Classes*, and *Nation*—culture, their work and creation, 109
MONTESQUIEU on liberty, 25, 27, 94
MOZART, 168

NAPOLEON and plebiscites, 123, 168

Index

NATION (see also *State*)—historical missions of, 82; not above men, 84; not acceptable as end for democracy, 152; natural structure, 154; its health defined, 188; organic nature of, 188, 193

NECESSITY —from individual end, 101; from social end, 113; rôle in selection of leaders, 113

ORDER—lesson of war, 19; defined, 90

ORGANIC DEMOCRACY—lesson of war, 19; its principles, 77; compared with totalitarian States, 148; methods advocated, 201; principles recalled, 211

ORGANIZATION (Spontaneous), 192

OXFORD and education of distinguished youth, 136

PARLIAMENTARY SYSTEM—degeneration, 70; instability of Government under, 71; causes of success in England, 212

PARTY SYSTEM—finance of politics, 71; no place for it in unanimous democracy, 148–153

PEACE—Conference beginning of downfall of liberal democracy, 17–18; eve glorious, 18

PEACE—International, 142

PEACE—National, defined as health, 197

PEOPLE—sovereignty of, 16, 39; misconceptions on government by, for, 38; defined as natural class, 156; man of, 160; defined by psychic features, 186–189; psychic changes due to modern inventions, 208

PHILIP II, 148

PLATO, 25, 34

PRESIDENTIAL SYSTEM, 70

PRESS—ill effects of private ownership, 66; suggestions, 231

PRIVATE INITIATIVE—value of, as principle of capitalism, 39; relation to private ethics, 40; to State, 120, 134; to inequality, 135

PRIVATE PROPERTY—and labour, 45; accumulation of, 136

PRODUCERS—tyranny of, 57, 61, 119

PROLETARIAT — defined in social scheme, 174, 178, 182

REFORMATION, 7
RELIGIOUS WARS, 7–9
REVOLUTION, 14–15
RICHELIEU, 159
ROOSEVELT (Theodore), 159
ROUSSEAU, 28

242

Index

RUSSIA—dictatorship in Russia, 13, 20; historical mission of Soviet Russia, 83; plebiscites, 124; aristocracy in Soviet Russia, 127; value of experience, 133; new ways, 174; unemployment in Russia, 176; bourgeoisie reborn, 176

SCANDINAVIAN COUNTRIES, 10, 205
SCOTT (Captain), 84
SELF-GOVERNMENT, 194
SHAKESPEARE, 159, 168
SHIPOWNERS, 18
SOCIALISM (see also *Communism, Labour, Working Classes*)—its success, 45; its theory, 130; its failure, 133; relation to private enterprise, 134; sceptic attitude about politics, 149
SODDY (Professor) on credit, 62
SOUTH AMERICA, 187, 202
SOVEREIGNTY—in old monarchies, 15; of the people, 16; misconceptions thereon, 39; State has sovereignty, 138; in internal economic affairs, 140; in internal political affairs, 141; in foreign affairs, 142
SPAIN—civil war in, 7; doctrine of State in old, 15; historical mission, 83; as totalitarian State, 148; self-government in, 194; tendency to corruption, 202
SPONTANEOUS ORGANIZATION (see *Organization*)
STATE—doctrine of, 15; rights reasserted by dictatorships, 21; irritation caused by its encroachments, 28; exclusion from economic affairs, 39–40; relation to business, 40; its organic nature, 50; statistical conception thereof, 50; development through technique, 56; weakness towards producers, 58, 119; subservience to economic forces, 60; evicted by bankers, 62; individual subordinated to State, 77; as background of individual, 79; definition, 81; rôle towards citizen and man, 85; justified only in function of citizens, 88; its right to limit liberty defined, 88, 116; relation to private ethics, 96, 117; to freedom of thought, 97, 104; to private initiative, 120; no right to be Marxist, 134; as economic and financial leader, 137; its sovereignty, 138–142; relation to world citizenship, 143; totalitarian State, 148; must be a true republic, 151; proposed constitution, 213, 222

243

Index

STATESMAN (see also *Aristocracy*), 159

STRIKES AND LOCK-OUTS—as industrial civil war, 57; as political weapons, 58, 119

STUDENTS brought forward by equalitarianism, 36

SUFFRAGE—evils of suffrage, 35, 50; discredited with Labour, 57; territorial or professional, 128

SWITZERLAND, 204

TECHNIQUE—invasion in modern world, 54; reduces citizen's importance, 55; increases area of State, 56; a bourgeois characteristic, 157, 165; demands evolution of type of leader, 208

TOLERANCE, 121

TOTALITARIAN STATES compared to organic democracy, 148

UNEMPLOYMENT—symptom of economic hold on State, 60; in Russia, 176; suggestions, 221

UNITED STATES—one of hopes of liberty, 10; standards of liberty, 13; revolution, 14, 15; degeneration of political institutions, 70; lacking in "people," 187, 202; in aristocracy, 203

VITORIA (Father) on conscientious objection, 145

WILSON (President Woodrow), 17, 18

WORKING CLASSES (see also *Labour, Socialism, Strikes and Lock-outs, Producers*) — and class struggle, 45; attitude towards intellectual work, 51; incapacity to solve social problem, 52, 150; industrial civil war, 119; scepticism about politics, 149; divorce from bourgeois parties, 149; defined in social scheme, 173; not really a class, 175; extremism and skilled work, 177; overgrown in modern societies, 207

WORLD COMMUNITY, 209

WORLD PATRIOTISM, 210

YOUTH—tendency to Fascism, 14, 19

For Product Safety Concerns and Information please contact our EU representative GPSR@taylorandfrancis.com
Taylor & Francis Verlag GmbH, Kaufingerstraße 24, 80331 München, Germany

www.ingramcontent.com/pod-product-compliance
Lightning Source LLC
Chambersburg PA
CBHW071828300426
44116CB00009B/1475